Everything TO LIVE FOR

TURIA PITT
WITH LIBBY HARKNESS

WILLIAM HEINEMANN: AUSTRALIA

A William Heinemann book
Published by Random House Australia Pty Ltd
Level 3, 100 Pacific Highway, North Sydney NSW 2060
www.randomhouse.com.au

First published by William Heinemann in 2013

Addresses for companies within the Random House Group can be found at www.randomhouse.com.au/offices

National Library of Australia
Cataloguing-in-Publication entry

Pitt, Turia, author.
Everything to live for: the inspirational story of
Turia Pitt / Turia Pitt; Libby Harkness.

ISBN 978 0 85798 026 7 (paperback)

Pitt, Turia.
RacingThePlanet.
Endurance sports – Australia – Biography.
Marathon running – Australia – Biography.
Disaster victims – Western Australia – Biography.
Burns and scalds – Patients – Australia – Biography.
Skin – Wounds and injuries – Treatment.
Transplantation of organs, tissues, etc. – Australia.
Wildfires – Western Australia – Prevention and control.

Other Authors/Contributors:
Harkness, Libby, author.

796.046092

Cover design by Christabella Designs
Typeset in 11.5/15 pt Sabon by Midland Typesetters, Australia
Printed in Australia by Griffin Press, an accredited ISO AS/NZS 14001:2004 Environmental Management System printer

Random House Australia uses papers that are natural, renewable and recyclable products and made from wood grown in sustainable forests. The logging and manufacturing processes are expected to conform to the environmental regulations of the country of origin.

*This book is dedicated to the other two 'amigos' –
my mother and Michael*

CONTENTS

Map ... vii

Foreword by Michael Usher, *60 Minutes* ... ix

Prologue: Fire ... 1

1 My Life Before ... 3

2 Michael ... 17

3 The Run-up ... 30

4 The Race ... 36

5 The Aftermath of Hell ... 46

6 Delay ... 54

7 Miscommunications ... 63

8 Rescue ... 72

9 The Bad News ... 83

10 Intensive Care ... 99

11 Dark Days ... 108

12 The Three Amigos ... 120

13 The Organiser's Response ... 130

14 My Life After ... 137

15 More Milestones ... 151

16 A Life Beyond ... 158

17 The Ripple Effect ... 169

18 Holding Responsibility ... 180

Epilogue: Fundraising ... 201

About Skin Donation ... 207

Notes ... 215

Picture Credits   221
Acknowledgements – Turia Pitt   223
Acknowledgements – Libby Harkness   226
About the Authors   229

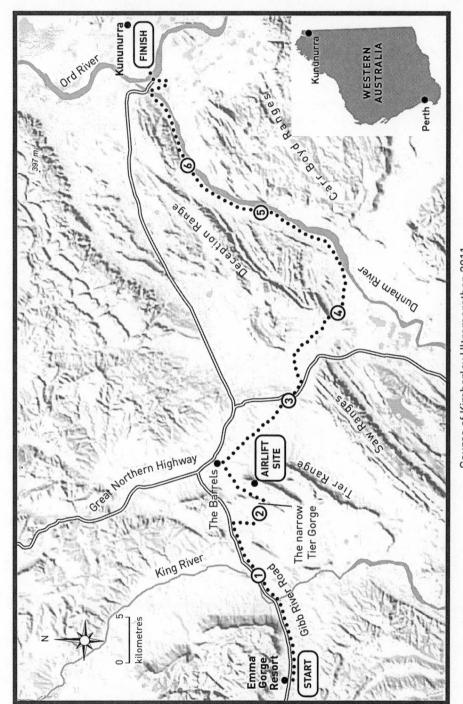

Course of Kimberley Ultramarathon 2011 (numbers indicate checkpoints).

FOREWORD

TURIA PITT IS THE STRONGEST PERSON I KNOW. SHE'S ALSO SMART, tough, funny and forthright.

Believe me, there have been times over the past two years when our interviews and conversations have turned around and suddenly Turia's the one asking me the questions!

That strength and willpower allowed Turia to become a survivor. And one of the most amazing survivors you'll ever meet. She shouldn't have lived through the hell of that outback bush fire: her doctors have never seen a burns patient live, having suffered such deep and severe burns. But Turia doesn't give up. It's not in her nature. She questions, she challenges, and she works damn hard to regain her independence.

None of us can really understand what Turia endures every day as she rebuilds her life. But I do know that she has my highest respect.

Her story is inspirational. You'll be embarrassed by your daily gripes and complaints when you realise what Turia goes through every day to rebuild her life.

I think you'll also find that Turia's story will challenge your own fears and insecurities. What happens when your looks change? What happens when your physical identity becomes something entirely different? How do you see yourself and how do others see you? Turia has had to confront all of this, and she has some amazing answers to these questions. Most beautifully, she's always told me that her burns may have been skin deep, but the fire couldn't touch her soul. And her soul is full of love, strength and hope.

I was nervous when I first met Turia in late 2011 when she was still in the burns ward. Those nerves didn't last long. Turia very quickly started hitting me with questions, we had a laugh and we became mates.

You'll also have a laugh with Turia as she tells her story. But mostly I think, like me, you'll be in awe of her spirit. Turia's story puts our own lives in some much-needed perspective.

Michael Usher, *60 Minutes*

PROLOGUE

FIRE

THE FIRE WAS COMING TOWARDS US SO FAST THERE WAS NO time to think. The noise was louder than a jet engine and I was scared. My heart was pumping. Searing heat and thick smoke were stressing me more.

I didn't know the others; I told one of them that I was scared and he said not to worry, that if we hid behind the rocks halfway up the hill the fire would just go over us.

There was no way out; I knew I had to go up; I also knew fire went faster up hills. The rocky escarpment was steep and covered in long dry grass. I had already run about 23 kilometres and I was pretty tired but I made it to the rock ledge with the others and we stood there for a minute as the fire raged towards us. It all happened very quickly.

I dragged a long-sleeved top from my backpack and tried to protect my legs with it as I curled up in a small depression among the rocks. But it just got hotter and hotter and hotter . . . I couldn't stand it anymore. Terrified, I stood and tried scrambling further up the hill and that's when the fire swept over me; I fell, and as I put my hands out in front of me, they were on fire.

I was screaming; I don't know for how long or how loud. I was screaming with terror and crying with pain. *Fuck, is this how I die?* At that moment the person I thought about most was Michael. *No, this is not how I die.*

Then I felt nothing. I don't remember much else after that.

Turia Pitt

ONE

MY LIFE BEFORE

ON FRIDAY 2 SEPTEMBER 2011, AT THE AGE OF TWENTY-FOUR, while competing in an ultramarathon in the beautiful Kimberley region of Far North Western Australia, my life changed forever.

I can never get my old life back. It's gone, along with my fingers, my old face and nose, the smooth skin on my arms, legs and neck; gone also is the way the world looked at me. The way strangers look at me now is different to the way they looked at me before the fire.

I was living the dream life. I was fit, healthy and happy; I had it all – a great family, a cool job, a fun circle of friends and a man I loved. I still have those things – the company I worked for even said I could have my old job back if I wanted it. But nothing is really the same. And never will be. I will have a disability for the rest of my life, and I am still young.

Let me tell you about the life I had before the fire.

I was born in Papeete, Tahiti, on 28 July 1987; my mum, Célestine, is Tahitian from a place called Faa'a. Dad, Michael, is Australian from Sydney. Dad was living his dream life – living and surfing in Tahiti – when he met Mum. She was sixteen, very beautiful and training to be a teacher. They married when she was seventeen; she had my brother Genji when she was eighteen and me when she was nineteen.

By the time I was born, Dad had been living in Tahiti for six years and, while he loved it, he was seriously thinking of moving back to Australia as he wanted us to be brought up there. He's a graphic artist, and when he was offered a good job opportunity in Sydney he decided to take it, and we moved there in 1988. I was eight months old and Genji was eighteen months.

When we first arrived we lived in the inner-city suburb of Chippendale, where I took my first steps at nine months. Mum says that even as a toddler, I was always active, always wanting to be on the go. She would walk us to Hyde Park in the city, Genji walking beside the pushchair, with me in it struggling to get out and walk too.

We moved to Maroubra when I was three and it was also about this time when we first went back to Tahiti. I was too young to remember much but Mum tells me all my relatives were so happy to see Genji and me. My *mamie* (Tahitian grandmother) says we may have been brought up in Australia, but our spirit belongs to the *fenua* (land).

I started school at Daceyville Primary in Maroubra; Genji was already there and I couldn't wait to join him. One of the main things I remember about my childhood is looking up to Genji. We were close, not just in age. I was always trying to tag along wherever he went; sometimes he'd let me, other times he wouldn't.

We were quite competitive though. I was always trying to outdo anything he did. He was hyperactive and not afraid of anything. Because we didn't have a telly, Genji and

I used to climb up on the roof and watch our neighbours' telly through their skylight. Once he tried to get me to jump off the roof but I wouldn't. I'm adventurous but I wasn't that stupid! We shared a room when we were young and I was more particular about my side of the room than he was about his and I drew a line down the middle that he wasn't allowed to cross.

I was into books at an early age. Mum loved reading and wanted to be a writer. To improve her English, she joined the Bowen Library in Maroubra and always had a big pile of books in the house. She and Dad didn't believe in TV, so we didn't have one for many years and we were encouraged to read instead. Every Friday night we would go to Bowen and select our books for the coming week. I loved books by Roald Dahl (and still do), and as I got older I would read books by Paul Jennings. Genji wasn't much of a reader but he liked the 'Tomorrow' series by John Marsden – more action.

Dad comes from a tight-knit family. He and his two brothers – all keen surfers – grew up in Maroubra but spent a lot of their childhood and teenage years down the south coast of New South Wales; his grandparents had retired there and the surf was good. Soon after we arrived from Tahiti, Dad and his brothers put a deposit on a weekender at Lake Tabourie on the South Coast, about a four-hour drive from Sydney. Dad liked the way the Greeks and Italians met up for big family get-togethers at weekends and holidays and he thought that was the way our family should be too.

By the time I was four, we were going down to Tabourie every second weekend and for holidays and we loved it. Genji and I would sit in the back of Dad's Citroën making up songs about going down the coast: 'Down the coast, down the coast, we're going down the coast . . .' We chanted this monotonously all the way there. We thought it was fun – it probably drove Mum and Dad mad.

Tabourie was where Genji and I first learnt to surf. Genji was really good right from the start. Dad would help me on the board and push me out into the waves but over the years I found Genji a better teacher – he was fearless in the surf. When I wasn't in the water or running along the beach with Dad, I was reading.

We had such a good time down there, no one ever wanted to go back to Sydney when the holiday ended. One day Dad said to Mum that we didn't actually have to go back. With the arrival of the internet, Dad's business had become portable and he thought bringing us up in a small community would be good for the family.

On the way to and from Tabourie, we would drive through Ulladulla, which was only a few kilometres away. Mum and Dad liked Ulladulla and so they decided to move there when I was eight. At first I wasn't very happy about the idea of leaving everything I knew in Sydney, especially the library. But we had a family vote and I was outvoted. Once we moved there I loved it and started making really good and lifelong friends.

Ulladulla is well known for its protected harbour, which is where the largest fishing fleet on the South Coast moors. It is a major tourist town and full of holiday homes. One of its annual attractions is the 'Blessing of the Fleet' ceremony on Easter Sunday, with a parade and fireworks, and it's very exciting. Everyone takes part in the parade, especially the kids, who dress up and ride through the town on the floats. The floats have princesses, and I was a princess on one of the floats once. Part of the festivities over the Easter weekend is the Blessing of the Fleet Ball; I wore a pale green long gown and I was partnered by a friend, Nathan Carlson. It was the first time I started to feel more like a young woman and less like a girl. Genji was there and so was his friend Michael Hoskin, who was the partner of another girl; even then I had my eye on him.

But the best thing about Ulladulla is its beautiful beaches and great surf. Growing up, I was athletic and a bit of a tomboy and lived outdoors; we were encouraged to be active – swimming, surfing, bike-riding, running. Genji and I were both in the school swimming squad.

Mum and Dad bought a great house on a cliff over-looking the ocean. Dad, Genji and I would get up early and go down to the beach below and check the surf; if it was good, we'd be out there. When the surf wasn't up, we'd go for a run then go back to bed before school. Sometimes, if the surf was really good, we'd be late for school. I have long legs and especially loved running; Dad, who was seri-ously into keeping fit, would encourage my running and if he didn't think I was trying hard enough he'd push me to do better. Sometimes I'd be stung to tears but I was always determined and I never gave up trying to improve whatever I was doing.

When we first moved to Ulladulla it was just Mum, Dad, Genji and me. When I was nine, Mum had my younger brother Heimanu and then two years after that she had my brother Toriki. They were such cute babies and I loved them – I was their big 'Sissy'.

Mum started writing seriously in Ulladulla. She writes under her maiden name, Célestine Hitiura Vaite, and when she wrote her first book, *Breadfruit*, I was twelve; she used to give me chapters to read as she did them because she wanted to make sure her English was correct. When she wrote her second book, *Frangipani*, she didn't give me chapters to read. That book won a lot of literary awards and I was very proud of her. She also dedicated that book to me (*I'm returning the favour, Mum!*).

Genji and I started high school at Ulladulla High. Back then, there were probably about 800 students at the school and they came from all the surrounding directions. I hadn't been there long when decided that I wanted to go St John's Catholic School in Nowra; I have no idea now what instigated this idea but Mum and Dad agreed and enrolled me there. Genji followed and, being Genji, was popular straight away.

Going to St John's meant we had to make an hour's journey by school bus. When I was fifteen, the bus was involved in a serious accident on our way home. We were near the town of Sussex Inlet when a car crashed into the side of the bus, flipping it over onto its side. The bus driver kicked out the front window and we climbed out, but one boy was trapped and killed; he was the sixteen-year-old brother of one of my best friends and in Genji's year. It was awfully sad. Genji and I got out with just a few bumps and bruises but a lot of the other kids were injured and were taken to hospital.

Genji and I had a lucky escape but Mum and Dad freaked out and took us out of St John's. The accident happened on a notorious stretch of road – windy and hilly, with cars doing 100 kilometres an hour – and they believed it was too dangerous for us to be making the journey twice a day five days a week. I thought it was a stupid decision because how likely was it to happen a second time?

I was extremely pissed off about having to leave St John's; I loved the school and had lots of friends there. Genji went back to Ulladulla High and my parents put me into the local Shoalhaven Anglican School, but I didn't adjust at all so I also ended up back at Ulladulla High.

I always loved school, especially maths and science, as they appealed to my logical way of looking at things. One teacher who stands out when I look back on my years at Ulladulla High was my physics teacher, Mr Christiansen. I loved his classes – he was so enthusiastic and passionate about science. I think he was pretty proud of me being the first girl from the school to get over ninety per cent in physics. One teacher I often clashed with was Mr Torney, my maths teacher. I was very stubborn and impatient in his classes. Nonetheless, I still managed to get the Noether Mathematics Medal (awarded to the top performing maths student at Ulladulla High) as well as come first in mathematics and mathematics extension. In retrospect, I can see that a large part of my success in maths was due to Mr Torney's influence.

I guess I always wanted to make a difference in the world, though I didn't know how. Once in class the teacher asked us, if we could choose any magazine we would like to be on the cover of, what would it be; and while a lot of my classmates said *Cleo* or *Cosmo*, I said I wanted to be on the cover of *New Scientist* for discovering something that was going to be meaningful to society. Mum tells people I wanted to be prime minister; I dispute this.

I met Kristen Briggs, whom we all now call just 'Briggs' and Nicola Tucker at high school. We became close in our later years of school. Although we are all very different, we share the same attributes – drive, determination and ambition.

In my younger years at high school I wanted to be a doctor. I'm not sure what changed my mind – possibly knowing that it was what Mum wanted, and when you're young you have a tendency to rebel.

I studied really hard for my Higher School Certificate (HSC) and got a score of 93, which was enough to get me into engineering at university. Choosing engineering was the logical conclusion after my logical selection process. I wrote down the things I was good at and what I wanted from a job, such as career prospects and the opportunity to travel. I was a bit naïve I think. Mining sounded cool – huge trucks and big explosions; of course I was to find out it wasn't like that at all!

I had aspirations about doing something that involved mining's impact on the environment. I talked it over with Dad and we came to the conclusion that I'd be able to do more about the environment by working in mining rather than becoming a protester on the outside. I believe that mining could coexist with good environmental outcomes.

My eighteenth year was pretty big in more ways than one. Apart from sitting my HSC, it was the year Mum and Dad separated; at first I was angry with Dad, blaming him. But eventually I realised they were probably just not compatible, and they'd married when they were very young anyway. He stayed in our house, and Mum moved out but remained in Ulladulla, and my little brothers divided their time between them.

Because I started school at four, I was only seventeen when I left so I decided to do a gap year in New Zealand before going to university. I went to Queenstown in the South Island to work in the snowfields. I was sharing a flat with a Canadian girl called Nicole, who also worked on the snow fields. I liked snowboarding so it was a good way to earn some money and snowboard. I loved the lifestyle and seriously considered staying as I was having such a great time.

I had my eighteenth birthday in New Zealand. I arrived back at the flat where I was staying with my New Zealand flatmate to the biggest surprise – Briggs and Nicola! They had secretly flown over from Australia to surprise me, and when they jumped out – 'Ta da! Happy birthday!' – I was so happy I burst into tears. Mum had apparently planned to come too, but they persuaded her to let them come first. Mum got the message that it would be best if it was just us girls together and bowed out. Briggs and Nicola stayed for a week and we had the best time.

Mum did fly over later in the year to encourage me to go home. Mum, who hates the cold, stood with me on the side of a mountain and agreed it was very beautiful but pointed out how hard I'd worked to get into university; why would I want to give it all away? So I came back and enrolled in the University of New South Wales.

I did a double degree – mining engineering and environmental science (out of my interest in the environment). I loved university life and I was there for five years. It was tough but I went all out for it. I don't believe in doing things half-heartedly; you either do something or you don't. I got my degrees with first-class honours.

For the first two years I lived on campus but there were too many distractions for serious study so I moved out to share a flat with two friends near the university. But after a while I found flatting too expensive and I eventually moved in with my grandma, my father's mother, at her house in Maroubra. This was cool because I would travel down to Ulladulla at weekends to see my family and catch up with my old school friends. And Dad's family lived in Sydney and they would all come over for a mid-week dinner at Grandma's. Later I moved out of Grandma's and into a flat in Bondi with a group of Tahitians who were in

Australia studying English. I felt ready to know more about my Tahitian heritage and I jumped at the chance to move in with them.

I really loved my Tahitian friends – there were nine of them. We would make *poisson cru* (raw fish), play the ukulele and go surfing. I even invited them to stay with me in Ulladulla. Mum was so excited to meet them all and I was particularly happy when they told me how 'Tahitian' my mum was; she still wears sarongs twenty-five years after leaving Tahiti. I became prouder of my Tahitian heritage after living with the Tahitians.

I also started doing some work in my uncle's business at weekends to get some extra cash. He was in the stamp and coin business and we would travel to various stamp and collectors' fairs all over the place, sometimes even interstate. He sold the accessories that go with collecting – albums, tweezers and so on – which everyone needs, and we didn't have much competition.

I started modelling at uni to make some extra money. I needed to find a way to fund my planned travels. One job required the girls to wear swimsuits and high heels and as I walked out, I stumbled into the girl in front of me causing both of us to nearly fall over. It wasn't a good look and I knew there and then I wasn't cut out to be a model. Besides, I found it boring; it was also tiresome to travel to a casting only to be told you weren't pretty enough, tall enough, skinny enough. I thought I was just right.

While I was at uni I tried to go home at weekends as much as I could to see family and friends; Briggs and Nicola were still there and we'd party with local friends. And of course I'd surf. I got my driver's licence but I didn't have a car. Once, when I was about eighteen, I borrowed Mum's car without telling her and crashed it into the local

Kentucky Fried Chicken shop. When Mum saw the car outside in the morning with its front crunched in she was not too impressed. Sorry, Mum! I was still a P-plater and I lost my licence for six months, which I wasn't happy about.

I did some more meaningful things while I was at uni. I had always been interested in doing something to help children in Third World countries because no matter where children are from, they're still children and need to have food and be educated. My first participation in a fund-raiser for children was doing the annual 40-Hour Famine when I was ten. I was tall for my age, though fairly slim, and probably because I was so active I was quite strongly affected by hunger pains and felt a bit weak by the second day; Mum said it was okay to stop but I wouldn't give in. She says it's my Leo stubbornness – I was born with a small bump on my head and she calls it the 'stubborn bump'.

A friend who knew I was into projects to help children sent me an email about ChildFund International, a not-for-profit charity which at the time was raising money to help build primary schools in the Svay Chrum district of Cambodia. I called Briggs about it and she was up for it; 'Let's do it,' she said. Our aim was to raise $15,000 between us – $7500 each.

We found the fundraising hard going. A lot of people have no idea what goes on in Cambodia so it's not unreasonable that they ask why they should donate money; we had to stay motivated and motivate others. I was fitting in uni studies and Briggs now had a job in Sydney but we worked well as a team. We held discos and surfing competitions at weekends, and the money came in slowly. We would put our heart and soul into organising an event and would think it must have raised at least $4000 to find we'd only made $800! Our best event did actually raise nearly $4000, which we were naturally excited about. It was a surfing event called the Ocean and Earth Teenage Rampage. We managed to organise a deal where every dollar that was donated from the crowd, Coastal Watch would match. So the $2000 we raised was matched by Coastal Watch. Our slogan for the day was 'Help Phil Macdonald raise money for a school in Cambodia'. Phil Macdonald is a pro surfer and is sponsored by Ocean and Earth.

Also, we had a lot of local support: we got some corporate sponsors, several Rotary Clubs (Ulladulla, St Leonards, Neutral Bay, North Sydney and Randwick) agreed to back us and we had a donor's page through ChildFund.

When we got to Cambodia, as part of the fundraising awareness for the school we joined a group of fifteen riders cycling around the country, which was organised by Child-Fund. It was only 350 kilometres, which doesn't sound like much, but it was hot and the start of the monsoon season and the terrain was difficult – roads were muddy and full of potholes. On the first day we cycled 100 kilometres and that nearly killed us all. But we did it proudly wearing our ChildFund T-shirts. Briggs and I paid for our fares to Cambodia out of our own pockets so all of the $15,000 we'd raised went to the school.

We actually visited the school, which was a real eye-opener. Classes were held in two shifts because of the number of students. The kids were all so cute and shy. Briggs sat at a table with what we thought were five- and six-year-old girls. The interpreter explained that most of the children in the class were ten to fourteen years of age! We later discovered that the kids were so small as a result of malnutrition.

I was so excited about our ability to raise this money for a good cause I wanted to do more. I said to Briggs, enthusiastically, 'Let's set up our own charity.' Briggs was more circumspect. 'Let's wait.' That's quite funny now, considering she went on to become a professional fundraiser.

I was always compelled to make a physical contribution rather than just donating money and in my third year of uni I got involved with an organisation called Habitat for Humanity. It works in Third-World countries on community-based projects to help reduce poverty. At the time, Habitat was working on housing projects in Mongolia. Volunteers had to pay their own way and I joined a team of about fifteen volunteers who travelled to a small village near a town called Erdenet in Mongolia to build cement-block houses. We were there for three weeks, and it was cold and our accommodation a bit basic, but I loved it. We stayed in tents called *gers* and I was shocked when I found out how much a *ger* cost – US$5000! I guess that explained why there would sometimes be up to twenty people in a five-metre diameter tent. I loved the Mongolian people – they liked playing games, although they never quite got the hang of rugby league and preferred soccer.

Part of gaining an engineering degree is doing work experience over the three-month summer break. My first job was at an open-cut coal mine in Singleton in New South Wales as a surveyor's assistant, where I had to do pretty basic stuff like hammering in the pegs and measuring windrows. I liked it but in reality I was too caught up with partying with the other vacation students to get really involved. The following year I was at another open-cut coal mine – at Hail Creek near Mackay in Queensland. That was better as another work experience student and I actually got to do some engineering work such as drill and blast designs. The third work experience was with a mine consultancy in

Sydney; I chose this as I knew it would be my last summer in Sydney and I could be near my family and go home for weekends.

By this stage Michael and I were together.

TWO

MICHAEL

MICHAEL HOSKIN, KNOWN AS 'HOSKO' TO HIS FRIENDS, WAS Genji's best friend and three years older than me. He was a year ahead of Genji at school but they both lived for surfing and were always in the water. He'd come to the house with Genji and we were just mates; I knew he thought of me as 'Genji's little sister'. But I always thought he was hot, really sexy-looking – he is fair-haired, very fit and has a great body. I had a crush on him from the time I was about fifteen. I used to fantasise about us getting married and having kids together.

We'd be at the same parties but nothing ever happened. One night, after a party at my place when I was in Year 12, Michael had too much to drink and someone put him to bed in my bed. 'Oh goodie,' I thought when I saw him and hopped in beside him but I must have passed out too because when I woke up he was gone. This also happened on another occasion when I invited him to a party at my place. Once again he ended up asleep on my bed and once again nothing happened. At my twenty-first we got around to telling each other how much we liked each other but it didn't go further.

Michael grew up a few kilometres from Ulladulla in a place called Narrawallee. His parents, Gary and Julie, are really cool and he has a younger brother, Aaron, and sister, Shae. After he left school he went overseas for a while and when he came back he joined the New South Wales Police Force. He was stationed at Maroubra, where I was living with my grandma, and I'd sometimes inadvertently run into him. We never dated then but I always had Michael at the back of my mind.

In 2009 Mum got married again – to a local guy, John Macguire, a former New South Wales representative rugby league player. He was a widower whose wife had died of cancer when they were living in France, where he was playing rugby league for different clubs. He had a daughter, Victoria, who was in the same year as Genji at school. John worked as a carer at a nursing home in nearby Milton, which is probably a good indicator of his nature. They had a big, traditional Tahitian wedding and I was very happy for Mum. They had bought a cottage overlooking Lake Burrill, which is five minutes from Ulladulla. The following year Dad also remarried. Dad and Karen had an intimate and lovely wedding at McKell Park, at Sydney's Darling Point.

After uni finished at the end of 2009, I went home to Ulladulla for a few weeks' break before starting my work placement in the New Year. I met up with Briggs and some other friends and they told me there was a party on. I will never forget the date: Friday 11 December. When I came out of my bedroom wearing a white skirt over a blue leotard and with my long hair out, Mum said, 'Woo hoo, you look hot tonight. Are you going to kiss anyone?'

'Only if Michael Hoskin is there,' I said. I'd had enough of something almost happening so I thought, 'Tonight I'm going to kiss him.'

He was there. I told Briggs that 'tonight was the night'. And it was. I kissed him and told him I wanted to have his children. He laughed but in a nice way. One of the things I liked about him was that he was so low key and casual. It was a great night and I ended up going back to his place on the proviso that there was no funny business. I remember waking up in the morning feeling just so happy that we'd finally got together. When he dropped me off at Mum's later, he said he would phone me from Sydney on Tuesday. I waited all day on Tuesday, my heart sinking as the day went on, thinking he was not going to call. He finally phoned at 8 o'clock that night. And that was the beginning.

The next year was extra busy but great. Michael was living in Cronulla with a couple of flatmates. I was again finding flatting too expensive and I moved from Bondi back to Grandma's in March. I get on quite well with my grandma – she is an intelligent old duck with impeccable taste. I also found her house to be a good break from flatting with friends. Furthermore, it was only a couple of blocks away from Maroubra Beach.

I had some bad luck with cars that year. I'd bought a Holden Commodore but it got written off when a woman crashed into me. I then got a little blue Mazda 121 and that got written off when I ran up the back of someone when they stopped suddenly at traffic lights. I replaced it with another Mazda 121, a white one.

Michael and I didn't surf in Sydney because we didn't like it – the surf was better and less crowded down the coast. When Michael got his days off, we'd do the three-hour drive down to Ulladulla and go surfing or diving off his boat. He had an 18-foot cabin boat and we'd go out and free-dive for lobsters or abalone. We'd stay at Michael's place, which was just south of Ulladulla, but we didn't see much of anyone because we were so active. We'd come home and have something to eat and go for a surf; come home and have something to eat and go for a dive; come home have something to eat and go for a run. After dinner we'd be so exhausted we'd just go to bed.

It was a great year for travel. At the beginning of 2010 I went to Tahiti for a month to stay with my Tahitian flatmates, who had gone back for the summer break, and I spent some time staying with the family of one at a place called Huahine, which had some world-class surfing breaks. I also went surfing in Indonesia with my dad and my brothers that year. And I went snowboarding in Perisher with my little brothers.

Michael and I had our first holiday together in October. We went to Vietnam for two weeks during uni term break and we loved it. I was a bit worried before we went because it was going to be the longest time we had ever spent together. But we had the best time and being together seemed natural. When we got back I dropped Michael off at his place in Cronulla and he was going down the coast for a few days with his family; when he hopped out of the car he just gave me a quick kiss and said, 'See ya!' and I started crying. I was being silly but we'd had such a good time and I didn't want him to go.

In July I applied for a job as a graduate mining engineer with the Argyle Diamond Mine in Far North Western Australia. Argyle was an open-pit mine and is one of the world's largest producers of diamonds and the world's largest producer of natural coloured diamonds. It is one hundred per cent owned and managed by mining giant Rio Tinto.

Argyle was my first job preference, a decision motivated by a lecture I'd heard by someone from Rio Tinto in my first year at uni. I was impressed by how well the company worked with the traditional owners of the land and its environmental management program, which included a range of projects to prevent, minimise or remediate environmental impacts. Besides, mining diamonds was a bit different from mining coal, the only type of mining I had experienced and the mine was located in one of the most beautiful parts of the world – the Kimberley. I had never been there but I'd seen photos and thought, how good would it be to have a job there?

I flew up to the company's office in Kununurra for an interview, flying first to Darwin in the Northern Territory and then down to Kununurra – a forty-five-minute flight. The mine itself is about a three-hour drive from Kununurra. Argyle had a total workforce of around 500 people.

I was told I would have to get my Quarry Manager's Certificate so I could drive the big trucks. That sounded so good. I would work two weeks on and two weeks off. During the on weeks, I would live in accommodation Rio Tinto supplied at the site and during the weeks off I would live in a company house with two other girls who worked at the mine. The job ticked all the right boxes and I was pumped when I got it; I was due to start in January 2011.

When I got the job Michael had been in the Police Force for about four years; he'd been happy for the first two years but by now no longer liked it. He had joined the force for a job, not a career; he had in his mind that he'd have four days on and five days off – that was half a year when he could be down the coast or in Bali surfing. But Michael became complacent at work and didn't seem passionate or interested in being in the Police Force anymore – he came to loathe the night shift plus he felt his work had become a numbers game, where the only thing his superiors were interested in was statistics.

I got an indication of how much he disliked the work he was doing when I took some lunch in for him one day. Someone came into the station and I thought Michael was quite rude to that person. It was then I knew he really couldn't be a policeman anymore because this was not the calm and nice guy I knew who was never rude to anyone.

When I told Michael's parents that I'd got the job at Argyle, his mother asked Michael if he was going to Kununurra with me. He said no, which really hurt. Michael had enrolled in a Bachelor of Education for primary school teaching, which was to commence the following term at Wollongong University. His idea was that we could see each other during my off weeks, and we could travel overseas during his ten weeks' holiday a year. However, by the time I started at Argyle, management had changed and so had my job; they were short-staffed and I was not driving trucks as I was needed for other work in the office. That also meant my roster would not be two weeks on and two weeks off. I had normal weeks, with a three-day weekend every second week. That put paid to Michael's plan for us to see each other during my off weeks.

In the end he decided he didn't want to teach kids; again he was choosing time off over a career. He resigned from the Police Force and made a snap decision to join me in Kununurra, go to the mines and see what happened. I was pretty happy with that decision. So the day after he left the force he flew to Kununurra.

By the time Michael left Sydney to join me, I had been in Kununurra for three months and I was loving the lifestyle. Kununurra is located at the eastern extremity of the Kimberley region, about 37 kilometres from the Northern Territory border. It's quite a new town, initially established to service the Ord River Irrigation Scheme in the late 1960s, and its population is still only about 7000. Today, the locals work mainly in the mines or in various government departments.

Rio Tinto had shipped all my things to Kununurra, including my car, but the little Mazda was not really suitable for the outback. I sold it soon after I arrived and bought a Holden Rodeo four-wheel drive to get me to and from Kununurra and the mine.

I was finding the work stimulating; my first task at the mine was a million-dollar project to come up with a way to house the mining waste – waste rock is rock that is not ore. I really liked the people I worked with. I was in the technical services division and I was the only girl on the team but the ratio of men and women overall was pretty even. There were a lot of girls in the environmental department and also occupational health and safety (OH&S). The accommodation was flash – not new but I had my own room with kitchen and bathroom. There was also a gym and a pool.

I couldn't wait for Michael to get there so I could show him around and introduce him to the life too, so I was very excited as I waited for his plane to land at the tiny Kununurra Airport.

There is only one daily regional flight from Darwin and it arrives late morning. When Michael stepped out onto the tarmac, the temperature was already about 37 degrees: talk about a warm welcome! Personally, I thrived in the hot temperatures. I ended up buying an inflatable kiddies pool to cool off in, and I would sit in it on really hot days reading *National Geographic* magazine. Michael would stay indoors with the air-conditioning on. But the majority of the time we would be out camping so we would normally have a nice waterhole to cool off in.

My two housemates in Kununurra were Mary Kavanagh and Elle MacNamara. Mary worked in OH&S and Elle was in human resources. Michael moved in with us. It only took Michael about three weeks to get a job as a technician at a local mine about half an hour from Argyle. There was a bit of computer work but the job mainly involved grading different types of iron ore and working outside and he loved it.

He was working a twelve-hour day, 5 am to 5 pm, two weeks on (living in on-site accommodation) and two weeks off in Kununurra. Sometimes Michael would drive over to spend a night with me at the Argyle mine but because he had to start work so early, he'd have to leave at 3.30 am.

We managed to synchronise our time off together and we had so much fun. While we naturally missed the surf, there were so many other things to do. So the car would be packed and off we'd go. We went to the Bungle Bungles, El Questro, Home Valley, Halls Creek . . . we saw it all. When Michael was at work I would socialise in town with my friends, but I always missed Michael.

Once a whole team of about ten of us went out to a place called Andy's Chasm; we did a long slog over several hours climbing a steep cliff because I wanted to go to Andy's via the back way. After we found the back entrance, we had to make our way down the chasm using ropes and traversing slippery sides and deep holes. I was really proud of Michael as he helped all the girls get through the chasm; I remember thinking, what a great bloke.

On my long weekends, I'd finish work at midday on Friday and we'd take off somewhere. Michael's attitude was much more laid-back than mine; he'd be 'Let's see what happens' but I'm a very organised person so I'd be planning weeks in advance where we would go. Our lives were jam-packed with things to do.

We were both fit and healthy and spent our time off exploring the area around the Kimberley – the scenic hills, ranges and pretty gorges with their deep green and blue waters. We'd go camping in the 350-million-year-old Bungle Bungles massif (large mountain mass) or in El Questro, a million-acre wilderness park and working cattle station. We went to Falls Creek; we'd swim and fish in waterholes and waterways and lie under wild orange sunsets. We went over to the tiny coastal town of Wyndham to visit the crocodile farm, about an hour's drive from Kununurra, and we even flew down to Perth for a weekend to look for an investment property to buy.

Michael's parents, Gary and Julie, came over to Kununurra for a holiday and we took them to the El Questro Wilderness Park; we had booked them a tented cabin at the Emma Gorge Resort right on the edge of the natural bush and by a beautiful crystal clear creek. They really loved it. Michael and I thought we would be able to just roll out our swag outside the cabin but the resort was classier than that and camping under the stars wasn't allowed! So we ended up sleeping on the single beds meant for kids in Julie and Gary's cabin. This was the first time I really got to know Michael's parents and I was really stoked that I got on with my future parents-in-law so well.

I was getting involved in other activities in the town. When I arrived I'd volunteered for the local ambulance service. Because Western Australia is such a vast state, it relies on volunteer ambos in rural areas, and I started as a driver. Kununurra had three ambulances and only one full-time ambulance officer. One of the other volunteers was a girl called Bonny Rugendyke, and we became friendly after we were only ever rostered on at the same time. At the mine I also undertook Emergency Response Team (ERT) training that equips people for fire and other emergency situations.

I met a whole bunch of new people when I joined a group called Hash House Harriers, which went walking around the district on Sundays; that was a lot of fun. They gave members stupid names and on my fifth walk I got the name 'Deflator' because my car had a flat tyre on my way to the starting point. I went walking with the Harriers on the Sundays when Michael was working. When he was off we'd spend the time doing something together.

One day I got a phone call from Genji in Sydney. He had joined the Army after he left school and had been living in Darwin until just a couple of months before I moved to Kununurra. He'd left the Army and joined the Navy as a clearance diver. Genji asked me for the phone numbers of my two uncles, Dad's brothers, in Sydney.

'Yeah, why?' I asked.

'I want to borrow some cufflinks.'

'What do you need cufflinks for?'

'I'm getting married today.'

'Oh, okay,' I said, a bit stunned. I knew he'd met Angela, who was English, when he was in Darwin, and she'd moved to Sydney with him, but I hadn't expected this – I think they were unofficially engaged but I hadn't thought about a wedding. I gave him the numbers and said, 'That's cool, tell me more.'

'Sorry, can't Sis. Gotta go. Bye.'

I rang Michael and said, 'Guess what – Genji's getting married today!'

'Cool. Good on him,' Michael replied. That was a typical easygoing comment from Michael.

'Why didn't they invite us?' I said. I would have flown down had I known.

'Don't worry about it; that's just Genji and that's how he does things. Spur of the moment.'

At first I was a little miffed. The wedding was a small affair, with only two of Genji's mates and their girlfriends. But then I thought people should have the wedding they want and it was not up to me to decide how Genji had his wedding.

I know Mum was a bit sad not to have been there too, but she came to the same conclusion: 'That's Genji.'

Before we moved to Kununurra, Michael and I were heavily into fitness and would run and go to the gym together, and we started going on longer runs together after he came to Kununurra. I'm not sure why I loved running so much. I've heard people describe is at boring or that it hurts their knees and so on. Not me – I always found it exhilarating. I used to love running from the mine to the mine camp, back to the mine and back to the mine camp again. This was roughly 30 kilometres and the time it took would vary from three to four hours. I always knew when I had run late because the mess would be closed and I would miss dinner. The sun would normally set as I was running, which was beautiful; after that I would continue running with my headlamp on. Mostly I relaxed and listened to my music on my iPod but there were a couple of times when I was scared. Once I saw a huge python slithering across the road; it was bloody massive – it was as long as the width of the road and I couldn't even see its head or tail! I consoled myself with the thought that pythons weren't poisonous but I still ran home in extra fast time.

Another time I took my headphones out because I swore I could hear dingoes. As I started running faster, my headlamp caught a couple of dingoes. After we had a stare-off, for what felt like ages but was probably only a few seconds, I took off quickly, telling myself that if dingoes did attack, they would be more likely to choose a smaller target.

I also ran in town on the weekends but I enjoyed the runs out on the mine more – less traffic and more of a feeling of isolation. After my hard work at uni, I decided that 2011 was the year I was going to start pushing myself and start competing in events.

I was probably more into competing anyway, especially if it involved running; I'd already done a mini-triathlon (swimming, cycling, running), in which I'd come second, and a half-marathon (21 kilometres) locally, in which I came first, when I came across a promotion for the Racingthe-Planet 100-kilometre ultramarathon in the Kimberley on 2 September.

I checked out the organisers online: it was a Hong Kong-based company which had previously organised thirty-three foot races in various challenging places around the world, such as The Gobi Desert March, and ultra-events in the Sahara and Antarctica. It had also put on a 250-kilometre staged, seven-day event in the Kimberley the year before. I sent them an email indicating my interest in competing.

It was a couple of months before the event, and I emailed Michael and said I wanted to push myself and do it. He was not enthusiastic about the idea; he was doubtful that my fitness was up to it; I disagreed and our emails about this went back and forth.

As it transpired, after my initial enthusiasm my interest waned because I thought the entry fee of $1500 was a bit steep. It would be better to put the money towards the holiday to Tahiti that Michael and I were planning so he could see where I was born and check out the great surf. I stopped pushing Michael about competing because I'd decided I didn't want to do it.

A couple of weeks later I got an email from the organisers offering me free entry into the event. I was told that the event was being filmed as part of a sponsorship arrangement between Tourism WA and RacingthePlanet to promote the Kimberley region of Western Australia. Having me compete as a 'local' would be good for the promotion. What I didn't know was that according to the sponsorship agreement with Tourism WA, RacingthePlanet had to have a minimum of forty entrants.[1] They may have fallen short because I later found out that several people had free entry, and some of them were not locals.

My enthusiasm was reignited but now Michael and I were at loggerheads over it again. Then one day after he got yet another email from me arguing my case, he went out into the mine and thought about it carefully. He knows how tenacious I am and that if I wanted to do it, I'd go ahead and do it anyway. He is a peaceable person and hates arguments, so he sent me an email saying if I really wanted to do it he would support me. I was very excited. Wow.

THREE

THE RUN-UP

TEN DAYS BEFORE THE RACE, MICHAEL AND I CAME BACK TO Ulladulla for a break and to attend my graduation in Sydney. We had a great time with family and friends, surfing and going for runs around the local area. The graduation was a week before the race and we drove up to Sydney with my mum. Dad and Karen were in Europe – on a sailing holiday in Greece – and not due back until the following weekend so Dad missed it, but Grandma came.

I told them in no uncertain terms not to yell out anything when I came up on stage. Of course Mum and Michael whistled and yelled out, 'Woo hoo! Go Turia!' But I didn't really mind. I smiled, I was so happy I'd finally achieved this milestone. Michael told me later he was so proud of me. He said he'd looked at me as I went up to get my degree conferred and thought, 'She's got everything: great job, heaps of friends, fit, healthy, beautiful and she's about to go on this big run. She's killing it.'

We spent the next few days in Ulladulla. Michael planned to stay on for another couple of days as he wanted to go to a friend's party in Sydney which was the night before the race. He was going to fly back to Darwin on Friday afternoon and down to Kununurra on Saturday morning, where I'd meet him at the airport and we'd spend the rest of the weekend celebrating me completing the race.

Michael drove me to the bus station in Bombaderry, about an hour from Ulladulla; we were running a bit late and the bus was waiting. I leapt out of the car and tore off, giving him a quick kiss before getting on the bus and waving to him out the window. That was the last time Michael saw the old me.

RacingthePlanet staff held a compulsory pre-race briefing with competitors the day before the race in which they went over the course, cut-off times and mandatory and optional equipment to go into our packs. We were told there were six checkpoints between the start at Emma Gorge and the finish in Kununurra. The on-road route would be marked by blue bunting, and waist-high pink bunting would mark trees or rocks to guide the off-road route; the height was to make the route visible for competitors above the long spinifex grass that grew through vast parts of the course.

The event was to be filmed on the ground and from a helicopter by a company called Beyond Action as part of an action documentary film series. It was part of a tourism campaign for Western Australia.

We were also told that there would be no mobile phone coverage and limited satellite phone coverage and given a simple map of the region.

That night I was alone in the house as Mary and Elle were still out at Argyle. But I was very excited and busy getting my pack prepared. Compulsory stuff included things like a headlamp and back-up light source (in case we were still running at night), a red flashing light, compression bandages, a survival blanket – made of alfoil and also known as a space blanket – whistle, compass, blister kits, a certain amount of energy food, a long-sleeved top (for cooler temperatures in the evening), salt tablets and enough water containers to hold three litres. Anti-inflammatory tablets and treatments for mild pain relief, such as ibuprofen, aspirin and paracetamol – for head and foot aches – were also on the list. I didn't expect to be footsore as I would be wearing my light, flexible, flat-soled joggers but I tossed in some Panadol anyway.

Next morning the competitors met at about 6.20 am outside the local pub, where we were to catch the bus to the race start, planned for 8 am. The drive was more than 100 kilometres, to the Emma Gorge airstrip on El Questro pastoral station. The competitors were from all over Australia and about a dozen had come from overseas. Being a naturally chatty person, I became friendly with three guys on the bus who were working for Newcrest Mines, which mines gold and copper in the Pilbara in Western Australia. They told me they were staying on in Kununurra for a couple of days after the race and as they'd never been to the region before I offered to take them back out to El Questro with Michael the next day and show them around. I was rather proud to be living in such a place and happy to play host.

I tried to ring Michael while I still had mobile coverage but the calls kept going to message bank. The race was half an hour late starting so I kept trying. I rang him again just before the race started at 8.30 am but no answer; there is a two-hour difference between Western Australia and New South Wales so it would have been close to 10.30 am in Sydney. I badly wanted to talk to him before the race and my messages were becoming increasingly cranky. I was thinking, 'He can't even pick up the fucking phone.' I knew he'd had a big night and was probably still fast asleep but I was nevertheless cranky.

During the briefing before the race start we were advised to take at least two litres of water, so we milled around at the starting checkpoint getting our names and race numbers checked off and filling up our water bottles. The course director, Samantha Fanshawe, drew our attention to the scenery and said it was a 'shame about a little bit of a haze'. We had seen a few spot fires while driving to the race start and she said it was a reminder to be careful of them and to use our common sense and not go 'running towards them'. There was no more information about fires and what we should do if we came across one but she gave us some more instructions about course markers and cut-off times.[1]

The race was started by John Storey, a local farmer and a friend of RacingthePlanet founder, Mary Gadams; Mary was also competing. John had been a volunteer for the previous year's event in the Kimberley and he and his wife, Ann-Marie, flew to Emma Gorge in their gyrocopter. Also on the airstrip was the media helicopter with the Beyond Action crew on board that we'd been told about at the previous day's briefing.

On the crack of the starter gun we were off. For about the first 10 kilometres I ran with the three guys I'd been talking to on the bus. But I was faster and eventually pulled away from them, going ahead on my own. After checkpoint one, the course veered off the Gibb River Road toward the Tier Ranges. It was rugged country, through long grass, trees and shrubby bush. I stopped for a rest and some water at checkpoint two which was at about the 19-kilometre mark, where other competitors were also resting and chatting, and some race officials checked off our names.

The next stretch went through the Tier Gorge, the most inaccessible and difficult part of the 20 kilometres to checkpoint three. I set off on my own. On the way I passed two other competitors, a younger guy and an older man, sitting under a tree having something to eat. I couldn't see the smoke from there and I had my iPod on and couldn't hear anything either. When I took my earphones out to say hello as I ran past them, I heard a noise and thought it must be trucks from the distant Great Northern Highway. I look back on that moment now and shiver at my unwitting mistake.

A bit further on where the route funnelled into the narrow section of the Tier Gorge with high rock cliffs either side, I had to stop running; I was walking and clambering over rocks and was climbing for a while before descending into a wide, flat, scrubby bush- and grass-covered valley with a rocky steep escarpment on my right.

I was running again, still with my iPod on, when suddenly I saw smoke from a fire in the distance; to me it looked like a low brush fire coming across the floor of the valley towards the escarpment on my right. At that moment it didn't look all that big but as I looked about anxiously I saw a girl and a guy who were obviously discussing the fire and as I stopped, another two competitors ran up; I recognised them as the guys I'd seen having lunch. Another guy joined us, and as we congregated together, we looked around for a way out.

Suddenly, the fire was metres away and we realised we were in terrible danger. We were trapped; the wind was rapidly funnelling the fire towards us and into the gorge;

the only way out was the steep rocky cliff covered in long grass on our right. I knew fire travelled uphill very fast but we had no choice – there was no other way, we had to go up.

FOUR
THE RACE

FIVE OTHERS FACED THE SAME TERRIBLE PREDICAMENT AS TURIA in those seemingly short minutes before the fire overcame them all.

Michael Hull, from the Central Coast of New South Wales, was a veteran of extreme racing and had participated in five of RacingthePlanet's previous events over a number of years: the Gobi March, the Atacama Crossing in Chile, Antarctica – the Last Desert, the Sahara Race in Egypt and the staged seven-day 250-kilometre run in the Kimberley the previous year.

Forty-four-year-old Michael, a sales executive with a telecommunications company, was in the United Kingdom to compete in a 100-mile (160 km) race organised by Centurion Running when he was invited to participate in the Kimberley event. Michael was staying with his brother, who lives in London, when he received an email from RacingthePlanet's race director offering to waive the entry fee if he agreed to be part of a documentary being filmed to promote tourism in Western Australia. He said it was put to him as a way of 'helping them out'.

Immediately after the UK race, Michael was planning to fly to the United States to be his friend's support person in another ultramarathon; he emailed RacingthePlanet back telling them that if he didn't sustain any injuries and felt up to it, he'd be a starter. A week after his return to Australia he was on a flight to Kununurra. He expected to do the race in good time and promised his wife and daughters he'd be on the plane out the day after to be home in time for Father's Day.

The previous year the ultramarathon race had been over the same route but run in reverse; Michael knew that in the first part of the Tier Gorge was a stretch of approximately 2 kilometres that was narrow and rugged, the only part of the course where there was no vehicle access – no tracks or trails. He planned to do an easy run to checkpoint two and walk to checkpoint three, by which time he would have warmed up and could start serious running.

As part of the agreement to participate in the documentary, Michael was asked to wear a special camera strapped to his chest, which he was told he could take off if he found it uncomfortable or the batteries ran flat. He decided to take it off at checkpoint two because he found it annoying; a decision, in retrospect, he regrets. At checkpoint two, while filling up his water bottle, he saw Turia and the four others with whom he would later confront the fire. He left just ahead of the others.

About fifteen minutes later, the father and son team of Shaun and Martin Van der Merwe passed Michael. Thirty-two-year-old Shaun had immigrated to Australia from South Africa in 2005. He was living in Perth with his wife and one child and working in a corporate role for a mining company.

His fifty-six-year-old father, Martin, lived in Ghana, where he worked as human resources manager for another mining company. Both Martin and Shaun had taken part in ultramarathons before. Shaun's had mostly been on-road in South Africa, and the Kimberley ultra was his first off-road race. Martin was well seasoned at multi-sport competitions, mostly in South Africa. He had competed in Iron Man events and ultramarathons in both running and canoeing, the Cape Epic Ultra – an off-road cycle event over nine days – as well as the Ultra Man, an ultra-distance event involving running, cycling, swimming and canoeing over one year.

Shaun and Martin had a 'bucket list' of things they would like to do together, which gave them an opportunity to catch up every year. They took turns at selecting an activity such as a marathon, fly fishing, canoeing or mountain-bike riding; this year it was Shaun's choice. He'd seen a documentary on RacingthePlanet and was attracted to the ultra in the Kimberley. He'd always wanted to go to the Kimberley and thought this might be a great way to do it; he and Martin agreed that they'd squeeze it in before going over to New Zealand for the Rugby World Cup the following week.

Competitors in the event had a choice of doing 100 kilometres or 50 kilometres. Martin didn't feel he'd had enough training to do the 100 kilometres and Shaun didn't care either way, so they registered for 100 kilometres with the option of finishing after 50 kilometres. Martin flew to Perth to meet Shaun and they flew to Kununurra together.

About halfway between checkpoint two and checkpoint three, Martin and Shaun decided to take a break and have something to eat in the shade of a tree. While resting, Michael came past, stopping briefly to say hello. Shortly afterwards, Turia also passed them and called out hello.

After passing the Van der Merwes, Michael had gone about 500 metres more when he heard a roaring noise and surmised it must be a road train on the Great Northern Highway, which he knew was in the vicinity but still some distance away. He didn't see the smoke from the fire because he was consciously looking down so as not to roll an ankle on the rocky surface and he was also keeping an eye out for the pink bunting attached to trees and rocks to mark the course. He didn't think much more about the noise until he went up a slight rise – and there was the fire, steadily devouring the route to checkpoint three.

Meanwhile, back at the top of the gorge, the Van der Merwes, who had resumed running, were passed by two other competitors: Hal Benson and Kate Sanderson. Hal, a thirty-six-year-old financial analyst from Sydney, and Kate, also thirty-six, a private investigator from Melbourne, had been friends for some years; both had competed in other ultramarathons but this was the first one they'd entered together. They'd met some years earlier when they were both volunteers for an adventure race in Thredbo. Although Hal had done ultramarathon runs before, he preferred adventure racing – ultratriathlons that involve a mix of sports, such as mountain biking, trekking and paddling, and which can last anywhere from six hours to ten days.

It was Kate's idea to enter the Kimberley ultra; she emailed Hal saying it was a 'once in a lifetime opportunity'. Hal didn't take much convincing and a few days before the event he flew to Perth to meet her and her friend Andrew Baker, who wasn't participating but planned to join Hal and Kate for a few days touring the region after the race. At the last minute, Andrew joined as a volunteer.

The pair began the race together but while Hal took it easy at the start, Kate took off ahead of him. He wasn't expecting to see her again but caught up with her at checkpoint two; she appeared to be struggling with the heat. Hal, who'd been in the Army for three years and was accustomed to serious fitness training, did not feel affected by the heat.

Hal and Kate left checkpoint two together and were a little concerned to see patches of smouldering grass from spot fires along the route. There was smoke on the horizon. They jogged on until they had to slow to navigate the narrowest part of the gorge. When Hal and Kate emerged from this part of the course they came down to the floor of the gorge – a valley about 800 metres wide – and could see the string of pink markers stretching into the distance, slightly above the waist-high grass and intermittent bush. Ahead of them and about 300 metres to the right of the course markings was another smouldering fire. They discussed the possibility that they might be heading into a trap because it looked bigger than the other spot fires. They could also hear a worrying roaring noise in the distance.

They kept going but the fire front appeared to be getting bigger and the distant noise had intensified. At this point, Kate saw Turia some distance away and she appeared to be running towards the fire, and thought anxiously that she was going straight into it. But Kate could see Turia had her earphones in and her head down and knew it would be no use calling out to her, plus the noise of the fire would deafen any attempt she made.

Hal and Kate stopped. The fire had started sweeping up and across from the left side of the gorge, gathering momentum, and would soon be coming their way. They had two options – backtrack and try to outrun the fire or go up the steep slope on the right side of the gorge; they knew both options were a no-no in terms of what to do if confronted by a fire; on the one hand, no one could outrun the speed of a fire and on the other, they knew fire travelled even faster uphill. They had to choose one.

The Van der Merwes had also come across some burnt-out spot-fire patches after leaving checkpoint two but it hadn't worried them as the scorched areas were quite small. Back on course after their break, they heard a distant roar; Martin thought it may have been a fire they'd seen en route to the start of the race, coming back the other way. Nothing could have prepared Shaun and Martin for the sight that confronted them as they emerged from the narrow gorge and looked down across the wide valley: thick smoke and, in the distance heading their way, a band of flame stretching as far as the eye could see.

Almost at the same time they came across Turia, Hal and Kate and within minutes were joined by Michael, who had run back after seeing the fire blocking his way. Now there were six.

By this stage the noise was deafening. From where they were standing they didn't have the best vantage point to see exactly what direction the fire was moving but judged it was coming towards them by the way the wind was blowing the smoke. They quickly canvassed their options.

Turia said she was scared.

'Don't worry,' Martin said, trying to reassure her. 'We'll be alright if we stick together.'

They thought they might backtrack and find refuge somewhere in the gorge but after about 10 metres, they turned around and realised this was not going to work as already the fire was noticeably bigger and closer. Martin was thinking about the Venturi effect – what would happen once the fire reached the narrow entrance of the gorge. Essentially, the funnelling and condensing of the flames into the gorge would create suction, and the hot air pulled in would accelerate the fire rapidly through the gorge; it would be like being trapped in a blast furnace. So they all quickly made their way back to their original meeting point, traversing a small dry river bed with no undergrowth but dismissing it as a place of refuge as it was not wide enough to shelter them from the flames.

In the meantime the fire continued to advance across the valley. Vegetation in the valley included gum trees, acacias, grevillea and spinifex grass. The grass is renowned for being enormously combustible, burning hot and fast; this fire was fuelled by a seasonally high growth of dry grass. And September is the hottest season in the north.

They had run out of options.

All they could do was head for the steep wall of the gorge to their right; they could see a rocky outcrop halfway up; it had less vegetation. If they huddled there, with less fuel for the fire, hopefully the flames would go around them.

'I'm going,' Kate shouted above the rumble of the fire and started off up the hill and everyone followed.

They all started running as the huge band of fire came towards them, forcing them up the cliff. Martin, Kate and Turia stopped halfway up on the narrow rock ledge, which wasn't as large as it had looked from below. They were joined by Michael and Hal; Shaun had to stand just off the ledge as there wasn't enough room for him. They looked at the fire now licking at the bottom of the slope where they had just been standing.

Turia looked at Kate and started crying. Kate said, 'I'm scared too but it will be alright.'

There was hurried talk about putting on the prerequisite long-sleeved tops in their backpacks. Kate grabbed her merino jersey and by the time she had pulled it on, she saw to her horror the fire was surging towards them. A hasty discussion followed about whether the ledge would protect them, whether perhaps – if they all huddled together – they could use their backpacks as a barrier. But as the fire raced up the hill towards the ledge each had to make a split-second choice.

Turia crouched in a depression among the rocks, pulling her long-sleeved top over her legs in a last-ditch bid at some protection. The heat was intense; the air was thick with smoke and the flying debris of burning embers.

Kate hunched in a small crevice in the rocks, poured the contents of her water bottle over her and waited for the fire to pass – except it didn't pass.

Shaun looked at his father and said, 'I don't have a good feeling about this, let's go.'

Martin's first thought was to stay put and he hesitated.

'Okay, Dad, I'm going.' Shaun took off. Almost instantly Martin turned to run after him but by then he could hardly see his son through the billowing smoke.

Hal was already heading uphill; as he turned around to tell Kate to keep going, he heard the roar of the fire as it leapt over the ledge so, knowing he didn't have the strength to go any further up the slope, he veered to the right and ran parallel along the cliff.

The radiant heat was burning and blistering Kate's skin and the fire hadn't even reached her yet. Kate felt it was like putting her hand on the flame of a gas fire but not being able to pull it away. Her shoulder was on fire and instinctively she stood up to pat it out; at that moment the flames engulfed her. She screamed in a moment of pure terror. *This is what it is like to die in a fire*, she thought. Kate began to run, and fell over on the rocky terrain; seconds later she heard Turia scream and knew from the pitch of her scream that she had been caught in the fire too.

As the fire enveloped her, Turia was having the same thoughts as Kate: *Is this how I die?*

Hal heard the panicked screams and thought, *That's the sound of someone burning to death. One of the girls is gone.*

Shaun turned around when he heard Kate screaming. He peered through the flames and could see nothing but the combusting spinifex and Turia trying to follow him.

The intensity of the heat had become impossible for Turia to bear and she'd stood up and tried scrambling up the hill after Shaun. She fell, hitting her head on a rock. He heard her screaming with panic and pain and turned around again to see her disappearing into the fire.

Michael, who had seen Turia fall, knew he was next. *I'm not ready to die*, he thought and made the decision to run back through the line of fire towards the already burnt area, tripping and gashing his leg on a sharp rock as he went.

Meanwhile Martin – scrambling up the steep gradient after Shaun – slipped on a rock and sprained his ankle. Partially shielding himself behind a tree, he tried to get his ankle to function; he didn't dare call out to Shaun – he wanted him to keep running and save himself. As the fire raced towards him, Martin heard the heart-rending, agonising screams of the burning girls below. When the fire was almost upon him he pulled his nylon compression socks down to prevent the nylon melting into the skin of his lower legs and, like Michael, ran back headlong through the flames, holding his hands over his eyes.

In the depth of the fire, one of Martin's running shoes melted off his foot, causing him to trip and fall again, spraining his other ankle, hitting his head on a rock, splitting his ear open and burning his right hand severely on a burning branch.

Shaun ran for his life. He too tripped, heard a loud crack and thought he had broken his leg but he kept running and jumped off a 4-metre-high ledge, tumbling down the cliff-side. He then sat back under the ledge. When he looked up he saw the flames reaching over the ledge but it was too high up for them to set fire to the grass below him.

As Shaun sat exhausted, shaking, heart pounding, he checked the GPS watch he always wore on his wrist when running and saw his heart rate had reached 216 beats per minute and he had run 100 metres in 15 seconds. He registered that his leg was sore but not broken. It was 1.20 pm.

Looking down he saw a steep cliff across an open valley with some green tree areas and realised he was in was another part of the Tier Range.

Sitting there, he felt lost and alone. He honestly believed no one could have survived the intensity of the fire; while he had a strong impulse to check if his father had survived he was scared – if he went back to the small rocky ledge, he was positive he'd find five charred bodies. He'd invited his father to go in this marathon and was wondering how he was going to tell his mother he'd been responsible for his father's death.

Eventually he decided to make his way cautiously down into the valley, where he might be more easily seen by rescuers. The fire had started ramping up through the valley in the distance; he descended slowly and found a clump of trees where he sat down and wrapped his running vest around his face to avoid being asphyxiated by the thick smoke.

FIVE

THE AFTERMATH
OF HELL

THE HELLFIRE WAS OVER IN MINUTES.

When Michael emerged he found he was between Kate and Turia. He first saw Kate, who was standing up with her back to him. Where her clothes had been burnt off, he could see skin and flesh literally melting off her. He didn't know Kate; she turned and looked at him, wide-eyed and in pain, and he knew she was in a bad way.

Turia was on the ground; she had stopped screaming but Michael couldn't look at her after seeing Kate. He could not speak; words would just not come out of his mouth and he collapsed in shock. His legs, arms, fingers and ears were burnt and he had a large open gash on his lower leg.

Almost simultaneously, Martin arrived back, having picked himself up from the smouldering ground and headed to where he had heard the screams for help. The first person he saw through the smoke was Turia, lying on the ground, silent; he saw she was still alive. Martin introduced himself and asked her name. To his relief she answered 'Turia'.

Martin's plastic water bottle had fallen from its separate pack holder and burnt out, even though it had still had water in it, and as he struggled to remove his backpack to get at more water, Martin was suddenly hit by waves of nausea; overcome, he dropped to the ground next to Turia. His legs were burnt to his thighs and he had burns to his right hand; his ear was also bleeding from where it had been split open during his fall.

Once the nausea passed, Martin tried to move Turia a little to make her more comfortable and gave her two Panadol tablets and some water from a container in his backpack. He thought about putting some of his water on her burns but judged that as the area of her burns was so extensive, it was better to save any water to keep her hydrated.

As the smoke cleared, Martin saw Michael, lying down some distance away, and Kate, who he saw was also seriously burnt.

A few minutes later, Hal appeared through the smoke and heat. He had run into an already burnt-out and blackened area, miraculously escaping the fire but suffering from smoke inhalation. Hal had climbed back around the hill, adrenalin still pumping, to see if anyone was alive; he was expecting to find bodies. To his amazement they were alive but the scene was confronting; he immediately saw how severe his friend Kate's burns were. Michael, lying a few metres away, at first glance didn't seem too bad. Martin – though clearly not in good shape himself – was administering to Turia.

Hal went to Kate and gave her Neurofen from his pack and tried to make her more comfortable. He asked if anyone had something soft for her to sit on as her buttocks were badly burnt. Martin gave them a sleeping bag cover from his backpack – it was thin but at least it was something.

Next, Hal checked Michael; he now seemed to be in a lot of pain. Michael's Lycra compression leggings had burnt into his skin below the knees so the extent of his burns was not fully visible. But he had no broken bones. Miraculously, no one had broken bones. Hal gave him Neurofen; Michael impressed upon him that he was able to manage his own injuries.

'Look after the girls, mate,' he said. It was obvious that they were in need of urgent medical help.

Martin sat with Turia, helpless in the face of the seriousness of her burns with his anxiety growing about the whereabouts of Shaun.

'How badly burnt am I?' Turia asked.

Heartbroken at this polite question in the face of her horrific burns, Martin couldn't bring himself to tell her the truth. 'You're okay and you'll heal well,' he told her, in the most comforting manner he could muster. Her legs were throbbing and she asked Martin if she could raise them and place them over his stretched-out legs. He helped her do this.

At this stage it became apparent to Hal that as the least injured of the five, he was the only one in a position to take on the burden of decision-making. They had survived; they didn't know where Shaun was; the fire had moved on. His priority quickly moved to the problem of raising the alarm. Did anyone know they were there, let alone that two race competitors were critically injured? They were beyond mobile reception and no one had a satellite phone. Assuming the organisers would be alerted when they didn't turn up at checkpoint three, there was still no way of knowing how long this might be. They didn't know how far the fire had gone or if the course markers were still there or even if anyone else had been affected by the fire.

It seemed clear to Hal that he was the only one capable of walking out, so he said it would be best that he went for help and Martin, who at least seemed to be capable of moving around, stayed and applied whatever first aid he could with the supplies they had.

'No, man; I will come with you,' Martin insisted. 'Two is safer than one in this situation.'

Hal was impressed by the stamina of this older man, who was obviously injured and in pain, and that he was prepared to walk maybe several kilometres for help.

But Martin was also becoming increasingly concerned about his missing son; finding Shaun was uppermost in his mind. If Shaun had not come back to look for Martin – which Martin was felt sure he would do if he were able to – then he had to be either injured or dead.

'Can you help me find Shaun first?' Martin asked Hal.

Knowing that Martin should save his strength, Hal told him to stay put and said he would go and have a look. Hal spent about ten minutes walking around the cliffs, blowing his whistle and shouting but heard no answering whistle or shout. He returned to give Martin the news.

'This is not necessarily bad news,' Hal said, trying to reassure him. 'He may have gone too far to be heard.'

By then nearly forty-five minutes had passed since their horrific encounter with the fire.

The terrible image of the fire engulfing Turia and Kate had been witnessed by other competitors. The three young men from Newcrest Mining – who Turia had chatted with on the bus and had run with for the early part of the race – emerged from the gorge shortly after the fateful six had congregated and were discussing their options. They were still too far away to see the group through the bush but they saw the fire; it was a confronting sight. Two of the mining men had fought outback bush fires before but nevertheless they found the sight of the wide sweep of this fire quite frightening.

The men, Brad Bull, Wade Dixon and Trent Breen, retreated about 100 metres up the dry creek bed, knowing they couldn't go back into the gorge or follow the creek bed out. Trent climbed up the side of the gorge and found a way to escape; Wade and Brad followed him up the escarpment. From their vantage point on this ridge they suddenly saw some of the others and watched, horrified, as the fire sweep up the hill, engulfing the girls, and heard their screams. They also saw Shaun running down the other side into the next gorge.

From where they were, it was quicker to get to Shaun first so they carefully made their way down through the steep, rugged terrain to where he was sitting holding his shirt over his face.

Relieved and gratified to see them, Shaun told them how worried he was about the others; his father was among them. It was clear that Shaun was in shock. The Newcrest men did not tell him exactly what they had witnessed. But they knew they all had to compose themselves for what might lie ahead so they sat quietly for a few minutes. Then they zigzagged back up the burnt-out gorge, each man bracing himself for the possibility of a gruesome find.

On the way Shaun's shoes melted on the smouldering ground but he ignored the heat on his soles and kept climbing, blowing his whistle, hoping. Suddenly, he heard the faint sound of Hal's whistle somewhere; 'Thank God, at least one person is alive,' he thought.

So, shortly after Hal arrived back and told Martin he hadn't found his son, Shaun appeared, followed by the Newcrest men minutes later. It was an emotional father-and-son reunion; both having thought the other dead, they hugged and cried tears of relief.

Next Martin told Shaun how bad Turia and Kate were. Accompanied by the three Newcrest men, they picked their way over the hot, blackened earth and stones to where Turia and Michael lay and Kate sat crouched over.

Shaun and the Newcrest men quickly assessed the situation and went into the emergency action they'd all been trained in as mine workers. They spent the first few minutes checking everyone. They pooled their limited supplies to administer dressings, Panadol and water to Kate and Turia. Shaun also gave Turia some ibuprofen tablets. Unequipped for serious burns, they nevertheless did what they could by soaking their crepe bandages with water from their supplies to try to keep the burnt skin moist.

This was the Australian outback; by this stage it was after 2 pm and the temperature was 37 degrees and climbing. Hydration was a serious issue; even pooled, water was limited. There were now nine people on the ridge and no one knew how long it would be before they were rescued.

It was obvious that the heat from the sun was exacerbating Turia's and Kate's burns so the Newcrest men, helped by Shaun and Hal, set about shading the girls by stringing up their space blankets and silk bag liners between sparse trees. It was decided not to move Turia but to build a shelter over her where she lay.

Trent, who had assumed a leadership role, compiled a manifest of the names and race numbers of everyone present. It was imperative that word get out about the seriousness of Turia's and Kate's injuries and about half an hour later, Wade headed down to the valley with the manifest; the plan was for him to walk back towards checkpoint two, blowing his whistle to see if there were any other competitors still on the course.

Trent switched his focus to looking after Turia, who lay uncomplaining, with the hot wind blowing over her. Shaun attended to Martin's injuries, dressing his father's legs with some crepe bandages. Fortunately Martin's rolled-down compression leggings and woollen socks had prevented his melted shoes from burning his feet and ankles but when Shaun poured saline water over his right hand, his father didn't flinch. Shaun thought he must have sustained third-degree burns, which would have killed off the nerve endings and probably meant Martin would lose his hand. Shaun gave him some juice but they had run out of pain-killers.

Everyone heard a very small voice out of the blue: 'Excuse me, please.'

It was Turia. 'Can someone please get the ants off me?' Turia had fallen on an ants' nest and big ants were crawling all over her.

It was decided to move her to the shaded area next to Kate. When Shaun and Trent first took hold of Turia's arms to assist her to walk, they were horrified to discover her skin peeled off to the touch and they quickly took her by her underarms instead.

Belatedly, Hal went into shock and felt incapable of even speaking. Once he realised the Newcrest guys knew what they were doing he switched off and commenced the wait for help, sitting between Kate and Turia, giving them sips of water and hoping they remained conscious.

Kate's back and buttocks were too badly burnt to allow her to lie down. She would sit for as long as she could then when the pain got too much, she would stand up. Hal was silently concerned about the girls' airways swelling up and although Kate did not appear burnt on her face, he was sure she stopped breathing a few times.

Shaun helped Michael wet his visible burn areas and then sat with Turia, giving her occasional sips of water. She spoke a little and several times asked him if her face was okay. It wasn't, but Shaun felt it was the last thing he could tell her.

Knowing that the Beyond Action helicopter was out there somewhere, the men placed space blankets across the rock ledge, hoping the reflective shining surface would attract attention if it flew near. Time ticked by and Martin raised the subject of their rescue again. Even though Wade had been sent to raise the alarm, Martin was still keen on walking out to get help.

'Dad, you're not going anywhere. Sit right there. We have to wait,' Shaun told him firmly, even prepared to forcibly restrain him if necessary.

So they waited. And waited.

SIX

DELAY

AS REVEALED IN THE 2012 WESTERN AUSTRALIA GOVERNMENT Inquiry into the Kimberley Ultramarathon, many people knew about the fires in the region that day.[1] So why did it take so long for alarm bells to be heard?

The first person to raise the alarm about the fire on the day of the race was John Storey. John had, in fact, been concerned about fires in the region in the days before the race. On 26 August, John had flown RacingthePlanet's course director, Carlos Garcia Prieto, over the region in his gyrocopter and had seen a fire in the Dunham Valley, which was part of the course. The following day he sent an email to the then president of the Shire of Wyndham East Kimberley (SWEK), Fred Mills, regarding the potential of the fire to impact on competitors:

'. . . The fire that has been burning in that valley has been allowed to come unchecked right across from the main road completely annihilating the country that they will pass through. Its present position and the rate of travel will put it on the track that they will be running on the Durham Valley on about Friday when they will be coming through. Even now the fire could be put out with two passes of Lance's plane. It will make great headlines in the paper when we see "International Race Cancelled due to disinterest by Shire". The charred landscape will make a good backdrop for the film's tourist promotion too.'[2]

John was not a volunteer for the 2011 race and was assisting in the preparation of the course as a friend. The committee did not establish whether RacingthePlanet sought his opinion about the potential impact of the fires or whether he discussed with them his view that the race should be cancelled if the fires were not suppressed.[3] RacingthePlanet did not change its fire risk assessment at that point.

As subsequent emails presented to the inquiry revealed, Mary Gadams and the company's event manager, Riitta Hanninen, asked the Kununurra Visitor's Centre (KVC) on 30 August who they should contact about the fires. Nadia Donnelly, the centre's marketing manager, advised them it was Tony Stevenson at the local office of the Fire and Emergency Services Authority (FESA). Nadia left a message for Tony on 31 August notifying him of the event and asking what should be done about the fires; she also spoke to Luke Bentley at the Department of Environment and Conservation (DEC) about the fires in the region. Luke said he would be happy to look at the fires but would need a map of the course. Later the same day, Tony contacted Nadia and suggested that the local hospital, chemist and St John's Ambulance be notified of the race. Nadia noted that Tony did not have a map of the course. Nadia emailed Mary on 1 September letting her know she had spoken to Tony of FESA the previous evening and he was now aware that Mary would be in touch with him; Nadia gave Mary Luke and Tony's telephone numbers and email addresses.[4]

It transpired that RacingthePlanet did contact the DEC but not FESA. They were later to explain they thought Tony Stevenson was obliged to contact them.

After starting the race, John and his wife had coffee at the Emma Gorge Resort and then set off for home in their gyrocopter, deciding to first fly over the route to wave to competitors. John believed FESA had been notified of the fires and had a map of the course. But as he flew over the east ridge of the Tier Range to the valley, which the course passed through, John was horrified to see that a large part of the country to the southeast was on fire and flames were racing up the northeast end of the range.[5]

Straight away he turned back towards checkpoint two, trying unsuccessfully to contact RacingthePlanet as he went. He then used his VHF radio to call Nathan Summers, the Heliwork WA pilot of the helicopter the Beyond Action team had chartered for aerial sequences of the race. He told Nathan to land at checkpoint two and tell officials that a fire 'coming over the range about 2 kilometres away will be on you in two hours'. He repeated the message twice.[6] John Storey was unable to land himself, as a gyrocopter is not equipped to land in rough terrain. At this stage John believed he had done all he could to warn the organisers; his fuel was running low and he headed for home.

But the bush-covered terrain at checkpoint two had made it impossible for Nathan to land near enough to pass the message on personally, so he landed as close as he could, which was on the other side of the Gibb River Road. He jumped out of the helicopter and shouted the message across to a member of the media team on the ground; this message was then conveyed to RacingthePlanet's event manager, Riitta Hanninen, at the checkpoint at about 10.30 am.[7] Nathan then resumed his job of flying the Beyond Action camera crew around the region, assuming the message would be delivered and appropriate action would be taken to ensure the safety of the runners.

John Storey's two-hour calculation would put the fire at checkpoint two by about 12.30 pm. The cut-off time for competitors to reach checkpoint two was 2 pm, which meant there was potential for competitors to be caught in it.

When the message regarding the fire was relayed to RacingthePlanet at checkpoint two, the course director, Carlos Garcia Prieto, was still at checkpoint one; it was here he noticed a large plume of smoke in the direction of the Gibb River Road section of the course. Video footage presented to the inquiry by Beyond Action showed two other smaller plumes, one either side of the main one.

Garcia Prieto then left for checkpoint two with the aim of monitoring the fire, which he believed was near the Gibb River Road. As he drove to checkpoint two he kept an eye on the Gibb River Road smoke and determined the fire was no danger to competitors, who were passing through without incident.[8]

By the time he arrived at checkpoint two at about 11 am and was given John Storey's message by the checkpoint captain, Dr Brandee Waite, who was also the event's medical director, it appears that the detail of the direction of the fire – that it was coming over the ridge – was missing from the message.[9]

Garcia Prieto's interpretation was that the message he'd been given by Dr Waite – 'There is a fire coming towards us and it may be at checkpoint two in two hours' – referred to the Gibb River Road fire and not a new fire. Neither he nor Hanninen made any attempt to determine the exact location, direction and severity of the fire as relayed in the message from Nathan or to hold competitors at checkpoint two until they had done so.[10]

Turia, Kate, Hal, the Van der Merwes and Michael all came through checkpoint two after 11.30 and, had they been held there, it's safe to say they would not have been trapped by the fire a little over an hour and a half later.

At about 11.40 am, Kate's friend Andrew Baker, Nathan Dyer, a reporter from the *Kimberley Echo*, and Hanninen left checkpoint two and drove along the Gibb River Road to a point in the course called The Barrels, about 20 kilometres from checkpoint three. From here they planned to monitor competitors emerging from the Tier Gorge. After they arrived at around 12.15 pm, competitors coming through told them that fire was getting close to the track; as Andrew listened to what the runners were saying he was worried; Kate and Hal were not yet among them and he could see the smoke in the direction of the Tier Gorge seemed to be getting thicker.

Hanninen told the inquiry she noticed flames and smoke but wasn't sure how big the fire was; she said her main concern was that the fire would burn the course markers and competitors would get lost.[11]

Garcia Prieto, along with another volunteer, Scott Connell, and Mary Gadams' husband, Alasdair Morrison, headed for checkpoint three to start putting up the glow sticks for runners traversing the course after dark. On the way Prieto saw a lot of smoke and flames in the vicinity of the course and, concerned that if the markers got burnt the competitors would get lost, immediately turned the vehicle around to head back to checkpoint two.[12]

About 2 kilometres from checkpoint two he stopped when he saw a local volunteer, Lon Croot, who was 'sweeping' the course with another RacingthePlanet official. (Sweepers are race officials who walk with or behind the last competitor; when the sweepers reach a checkpoint, the checkpoint officials know that there are no more runners coming and they can close the checkpoint. They are also a safety backup – so that if someone is injured, at the very least they will be found by the sweepers.) It was Lon's first time volunteering for an event like this. Lon, a thirty-two-year-old forestry worker, had been helping the RacingthePlanet team set up in the preceding few days and knew there were fires in the area. Everyone he was working with knew there were fires because they had to go back and re-mark the course in certain places after fires burnt out the pink markers.

Lon was extremely worried about the fires. Even though they were spot fires, he was conscious that if a hot wind got up, the fires could rage out of control very quickly and he had mentioned this to members of the RacingthePlanet staff. 'Aren't you worried about that?' he had asked them.[13] They were all racing to get everything set up and appeared not to be concerned about the fires.[14]

Garcia Prieto drove Lon back to checkpoint two and asked him to go into the area where the fire was to help the runners stick to the course; he gave Lon his GPS to help him find his way and some pink tape to re-mark the course if it had been burnt.[15]

That was at around 1 pm.

After sending Lon into the gorge, Garcia Prieto, Scott and Morrison headed back to checkpoint three, arriving at just after 2 pm. By then only twelve competitors had come through – this left twenty-eight competitors somewhere in the no-man's-land between checkpoints two and three.

•••

Two other competitors, Brenda and Martyn Sawyer, had arrived at the top of the gorge just before 1.20 pm; straight away they saw thick smoke and fire ahead. They then heard a male voice shouting from the valley floor, 'Don't come down. Fire!'

This call was from fellow competitor Ellis Caffin, who – with his partner, Dr Heather Scott – had seen a huge wall of smoke, which they thought was about 2 kilometres in front of them as they came out of the narrow part of the gorge. They had dropped down into the valley and were following the pink markers. As they walked along the dry creek bed they could smell smoke, and even though they had also come across several small grass fires earlier in the day, they believed that as they had not been warned about any fire, it was nothing to worry about.[16] About five minutes after exiting the gorge, however, the smoke was thicker and the wind was in their faces.

Heather was getting nervous. Suddenly the fire was massive and they could hear its roar. Ellis, a defence force helicopter pilot, decided they should climb the valley wall to a narrow ridgeline with less grass. Each wet a piece of cloth to wrap around their faces and climbed up. Within two minutes the flames had climbed the ridge to where they had taken refuge. They were then faced with no other choice but to jump the fire line at a very narrow break into an already burnt section – a split-second decision which prevented them from being burnt. The heat was intense; Heather, a nuclear scientist, was the most scared for her life that she had ever been.

It was at that point that Ellis yelled up the valley to the competitors behind that there was a fire and they should go back. After Ellis saw the Sawyers turn around, he knew they would be able to warn any others.

As the Sawyers started to retrace their footsteps, they ran into Lon and told him what they'd seen and about someone calling out 'fire'. They suggested he should take a quick look and assured him they would tell anyone else they came across to go back.

Although Lon was familiar with the terrain of the Kimberley, he was not familiar with this part of the course. He continued walking to see if he could locate the people who had called out 'fire' from the valley. When he reached the top of the gorge he saw the fire racing over the valley and saw two people standing as if uncertain what to do, and he realised they were in danger. He called down to them and they didn't answer, although in all probability his voice could not have been heard over the noise of the fire. Terrified that he was about to witness people die, he called out again and through the billowing smoke saw the man running and heard screams from the woman as smoke billowed over her. He was later to find out that the woman was RacingthePlanet founder, Mary Gadams, and competitor, Ron Rutherford.

Devastated by this vision, and believing he too might be in danger, Lon turned and started to head back as fast as he could until he collapsed with leg cramps. Fortunately, Martyn saw him fall and he and Brenda went to help; Lon told him what he'd seen and said they needed a rescue helicopter. Martyn told Brenda he would stay with Lon but for her to keep going and get to checkpoint two as quickly as she could to get help.

When Lon had recovered from his cramp he took off ahead of Martyn, anxious to tell anyone still on the course to return to checkpoint two immediately. He reached the checkpoint just after Brenda, who had already warned Dr Waite that people might be trapped by the fire and a rescue helicopter would be needed. When Lon arrived he took Dr Waite aside and told her that he'd actually seen people being burnt and heard screaming.

It was now just after 2 pm.

SEVEN

MISCOMMUNICATIONS

DR BRANDEE WAITE, AN AMERICAN WHO HAD WORKED WITH RacingthePlanet since 2005, first dialled 000 at 2.02 pm and was put through to Western Australia's Fire and Emergency Services Authority's communications centre in Perth (FESA Comcen). Following is the transcript of the conversation:[1]

Dr Waite:	Hello, yes this is . . . I'm in the Kimberley this is Dr Waite and I'm with the RacingthePlanet that's running through the outback here and we're at the edge of a fire we've got a couple of people who've been burnt. The fires came across them and they've been burnt; we need some help with the evacuation.
Operator:	So where are you actually; what's the address?
Dr Waite:	We're not . . . there's not an address; I'll have to get you the GPS coordinates.
Operator:	Yes.
Dr Waite:	We are literally in the bush.
Operator:	Are you at a campsite or anything?

Dr Waite: We are not at a campsite.
Operator: Okay.

There are some long pauses and talking in the background and Dr Waite tells the operator the 'GPS has now gone quiet.'

Operator: Okay, so do you actually need the fire brigade or do you need the ambulance?
Dr Waite: We need the ambulance.
Operator: Oh, okay, coz you have actually come through to the fire brigade so we are completely not associated with the ambulance.
Dr Waite: This is not the SES? [State Emergency Services]
Operator: Sorry?
Dr Waite: We are trying to contact SES.
Operator: But if you've got people that need medical treatment, do you need the ambulance?
Dr Waite: Yes.
Operator: So what do you need the SES for?
Dr Waite: Is that not the ambulance?
Operator: No the SES are volunteers who assist so you'll need to hang up and ring 000 again and ask for ambulance in WA. If all you need is medical treatment, they may call the ambulance; they may call the SES to assist them but they will be the primary person to treat if you have injuries.
Dr Waite: Okay.
Operator: Okay.
Dr Waite: Oh, thank you.
Operator: No worries, bye bye.
Dr Waite: Okay, bye.

While it could be expected that Dr Waite, as an American, might be unfamiliar with the territory and the roles of the various agencies, the inquiry raised serious questions about the operator's response; it found that not keeping Dr Waite on the line while communication was established to the right agency was a serious failure.[2]

After Dr Waite's unsuccessful FESA call, she phoned event director Samantha Fanshawe at checkpoint four and advised her there was an emergency and that people were trapped by the fire. Fanshawe then made her own call to 000 and was put through to FESA.

Fanshawe told the operator '. . . there are bush fires out here and there is a possibility that there are two people trapped in a bush fire . . .' She did not tell the operator that people had been burnt or needed medical attention.[3]

Somewhere along the communication chain, the fact that people had been burnt was lost; the inquiry heard this may have been due to a poor connection between satellite phones.[4]

Although Fanshawe was unable to provide the GPS coordinates for the exact location of the 'incident', she attempted to describe where they were. Unfortunately, she was unaware that the FESA call centre was in Perth and the operator was not familiar with some of the remote place names she mentioned in Far North Western Australia. Fanshawe said she would phone back with the coordinates. At the end of the call, she told the operator that they had access to a helicopter and asked if it would help if they got it to start looking, '. . . or is search and rescue done through you as well?'[5]

RacingthePlanet had an arrangement with the Beyond Action team that their helicopter could be co-opted as first responder in an emergency. But instead of contacting the

Beyond Action pilot, Nathan Summers, Fanshawe tried to call the Heliwork base in Kununurra to activate their 'back-up emergency helicopter'. Her calls were unsuccessful, again due to bad satellite reception. Regardless, Racingthe-Planet had not booked a back-up helicopter, declining the option offered by Heliwork the previous day, so there was no guarantee there would be one available in the case of emergency anyway.[6]

Fanshawe next called Garcia Prieto at checkpoint three and told him there were runners missing between checkpoint two and The Barrels and they needed to contact the media helicopter and get it to have a look. He told her the helicopter was actually there at checkpoint three; she then spoke to Nathan Summers and asked him to fly over the range and investigate the situation.

Summers took that call at about 2.35 pm.[7]

When Fanshawe rang FESA back with the GPS coordinates at 2.45 pm, she was asked how many people were injured. She replied, 'Two people missing. No one injured.'[8]

After their narrow escape from the flames as the fire swept through the gorge, Ellis and Heather made their way down into the valley, heading back to checkpoint two but also looking out for any runners behind them. They came across the two people Lon Croot had seen – Mary Gadams, who had burns on her hands and legs, and another competitor, Rod Rutherford, who had managed to escape and wasn't burnt. They bandaged Mary, after which all four started walking along the layers of ash back towards checkpoint two, looking for anyone in front of them who may have been injured. Everything was burnt – the pink course markers were burnt and the trees were still on fire.

Ellis and Heather were sharing their water with Mary, helping her drink and cool her burnt hands as she and Rod had used all of their water. Heather kept blowing her whistle to see if anyone responded and after about thirty minutes they heard a return whistle; several more back and forth whistles were exchanged and then they found Wade. They made their way towards each other and Wade briefed them on the injured competitors up on the ridge, stressing the seriousness of Turia's and Kate's burns. He also told them the group was short of water.

Wade handed Ellis the list of names and race numbers of the group on the ridge and Ellis gave him some water, then Wade started walking back towards the ridge.

Because Mary was injured, Ellis suggested that she and Rod should stay put and, leaving them with some water, he and Heather headed off for checkpoint three.

There were no trail markers and all Ellis and Heather had for navigation purposes was a rudimentary hand-drawn map of the course. Most of the trees in the valley were still burning and branches would suddenly drop with no warning making their trek nerve racking.

After walking for about forty-five minutes, they saw Summers and a member of the media crew, Nathan Tomlinson, in the Beyond Action helicopter. Ellis and Heather waved like mad, pointing towards the ridgeline where they knew the group of injured competitors were.

Summers quickly located the group on the ridge by the reflection from the stretched-out space blankets. As he approached, Summers could see people lying down; some were seated and stood up and waved. As Summers got closer and looked down he could see obvious casualties. He thought he might be able to land but realised as he hovered over the site that it was impossible because of the rocky terrain and trees; as well as being hampered by camera equipment attached to the helicopter.

While Summers kept the aircraft hovering over the group, the rotor blades raised clouds of dust and ash that settled on everyone's burns and as he flew off, they knew rescue was near but not near enough. But still, the sight of the helicopter lifted their spirits; rescue must come soon.

Summers landed on the only suitable area – some distance away, on the opposite side of the valley – and leapt out of the chopper to meet Ellis and Heather. Ellis passed on the information about the other injured people. Summers immediately sent out calls on his radio but could not reach anyone's satellite phone. Ellis urged him to get back up in the air, where reception might be better, as another helicopter was urgently needed. But the pilot was worried: the nearest emergency helicopter capable of winching the injured off the ridge was in Darwin, more than 800 kilometres away.

Summers' helicopter wasn't equipped for medical emergencies but he did have water, which he gave to Ellis to take to the ridge, and then he took off.

Ellis and Heather headed back towards the base of the cliff to see if there was any way to get the wounded down the cliff face so they could be evacuated.

In the meantime Trent clambered down the cliff to meet them; after he introduced himself he reiterated the grim news about the state of the girls. Ellis and Heather told him that Mary Gadams and Rod Rutherford were also waiting in the gorge for rescue.

Ellis and Heather then decided to sweep the valley back to checkpoint two to look for any runners who might have been behind them. They commenced the 5-kilometre hike through the narrow gorge and charred wasteland beyond, blowing their whistles every couple of minutes. They never heard an answering whistle.

To their dismay they found checkpoint two burnt out and evacuated. They continued hiking for another 6 kilometres to the Gibb River Road; they hoped to hitch a ride to checkpoint three and hand over the list of all the people stranded in the gorge who needed evacuation.

Once airborne, Summers got a call through to RacingthePlanet, advising them of the location of the ridge and asking them to urgently organise another helicopter and an ambulance. Then he made one more attempt at landing to get Turia and Kate off, but it was impossible; there was room for only one skid on the rock ledge.

As they watched Summers fly off, and now knowing there was no way a helicopter could land, the men wondered how they could get the girls down into the valley. There was some discussion about assembling makeshift stretchers from space blankets and broken branches; this was dismissed as too risky on such steep terrain because they could be putting the girls' lives in more danger if they dropped them. They would have to wait.

Time wore on but the temperature had not dropped much – it was still around 35 degrees.

Summers collected Dr Julie Brahm, RacingthePlanet's Australian-based medical assistant (a Canadian, at the time working for a rapid-response Australian medical team), from checkpoint three and flew back to the site; he hovered over the ledge while she jumped from the helicopter and ran immediately to the injured Turia and Kate.

Then Summers landed some distance away in the valley, where he made two broken satellite calls to Paul Cripps, the operations manager at the Heliwork base. He explained there were five people with serious burns who needed to be transported to hospital urgently. After that, he and Nathan Tomlinson walked back across the valley and climbed up to the ridge with more water.

Dr Brahm's arrival and the calls to Paul Cripps were estimated to have occurred at between 3.45 pm and 4 pm.

After receiving the 'two tourists missing; no injured message', FESA passed the information on to the St John's Ambulance Centre in Perth, which immediately relayed it to Sarel De Koker, the community ambulance paramedic in Kununurra.

It was then 3.04 pm.

As soon as Sarel got the message, he rang the caller's number that FESA had given him. This belonged to Samantha Fanshawe, who told him there were fires in the region and people were missing; she told him they were at The Barrels. Sarel, a recent arrival from South Africa, had only been in the job for one week. He had no idea where The Barrels were but when he looked at a local map, he saw it was in the direction of the Tier Ranges, and that was some distance from Kununurra.

In fact, The Barrels are a local landmark – 'local' encompassing vast distances in the outback. They are a large collection of randomly scattered drums believed to have once contained either diesel or tar used during the sealing of the original Broome to Wyndham–Kununurra road many years ago. The Barrels are where the road construction crews are believed to have had their campsite and are located off the Great Northern Highway near the Gibb River Road turnoff.

In spite of there being no confirmation of any injuries, Sarel took the precautionary measure of calling head-quarters to request an upgrade to Priority 1 status so he could leave immediately to allow for travel time. He called in three local ambulance volunteers, one of whom was Turia's friend Bonny, and by 3.15 pm they were on their way, driving one standard Mercedes ambulance and one four-wheel drive ambulance. Once in transit, Sarel called Fanshawe again and obtained more detailed instructions on how to get to The Barrels.

On arrival at about 4 pm, he saw a RacingthePlanet banner, the first time he became aware that it was some kind of event. Dr Waite introduced herself as RacingthePlanet's medical director and explained that there was a fire and competitors were 'missing' but she didn't know if anyone was injured. Straight away Sarel called the St John's communications centre and informed them it was a race, there were fires in the region and there were competitors missing.

Shortly afterwards, Dr Waite took a call from Fanshawe: the gravely injured runners had been found and access was by four-wheel drive only. Sarel quickly organised for all necessary medical equipment to be transferred from the Mercedes ambulance into the four-wheel drive ambulance plus a four-wheel drive vehicle belonging to RacingthePlanet and the four St John's personnel set off with Dr Waite at about 4.10 pm.

EIGHT

RESCUE

PAUL CRIPPS, AN UNASSUMING MAN IN HIS MID-THIRTIES, LIVED in Kununurra with his wife and baby son. Originally from the Central Coast of New South Wales, he took up the Heliwork WA job in 2006; he fell in love with the job and the challenges of flying in the outback. Much of his work involved flying tourists and miners around the Kimberley region and he never tired of the vast, magnificent landscape he flew them over.

There are no dedicated search-and-rescue operations in remote regions of northern Western Australia such as Kununurra; the remoteness means governments fail to see its cost-effectiveness. So anyone injured who needs rescue in a remote area has to go with what the nearest community offers. As far as rescues go, Turia and Kate were fortunate that Paul Cripps and his co-pilot, Bryn Watson, were available that day.

The first indication Paul had that there might be an emergency was a call he received from FESA in Perth at around 1.45 pm advising him of a broken conversation received from a Samantha Fanshawe via satellite phone saying some people had been burnt somewhere between Kununurra and Wyndham (a distance of about 100 kilometres). FESA told him they knew nothing of the event and consequently there was no emergency plan for it, and on the strength of so little information FESA couldn't officially request Heliwork's services.[1]

After FESA told Paul about its unsuccessful attempt at contact with Fanshawe, Paul also tried – and failed – to make contact with her. He then tried to call Nathan Summers by satellite and various VHF channels but had no success. Finally at about 4 pm he got the first of two calls from Summers about the burns victims in the Tier Gorge. Paul, a mild-mannered man, had been getting increasingly worried about that lack of information coming through. Now here it was. And people were hurt. His attention turned to getting help to them as soon as possible.

In his second call, Summers gave Paul the GPS coordinates and told him it was a very difficult location to access; he would not be able to land there as there was only enough room to place one skid on the ledge.

Paul called Bryn Watson, Heliwork's senior base pilot; his tone may have been calm but Bryn got the 'time is of the essence' drift of Paul's message when he was asked to accompany him as crew. While Paul prepared the helicopter, Bryn tried to locate the aircraft stretcher; being unable to, he called the ambulance communications centre via the 000 service, requesting a stretcher and any other necessary equipment and, if possible, a paramedic, to be brought to the hangar urgently. The operator didn't know anything about the incident or that the only full-time local paramedic, Sarel De Koker, was almost at the incident site by then. This was at 4.21 pm.

By 4.30 the stretcher and paramedic had not arrived at the base and Paul was seriously concerned about fading light – the six-seater Bell 206L was not a special search-and-rescue helicopter and was not equipped for night flying. But Bryn was a Queensland-trained advanced care paramedic and so Paul made the decision to leave immediately.

En route, Bryn phoned the Kununurra District Hospital and spoke to the emergency department, advising staff they were on their way to evacuate people with burns; details were unknown at that stage but they should expect patients at about 5.30 pm.

Once in the air Paul then told Bryn that the location of the patients was on a ridge with room for only one skid. Nothing was said but each knew what the other was thinking and they flew over the magnificent landscape that would soon be enveloped in darkness. At that stage Paul declared it a 'mercy flight' as the casualties' location was not a standard helicopter landing site (HLS). In the past Paul had carried out several medivacs, some in fairly confined spaces, but never from the side of a cliff with no room to land a helicopter; he knew this was going to be a tough and dangerous job and he was thinking how he could minimise risks to everyone involved.

Dr Brahm assessed the situation and knew it was imperative that the women receive immediate intravenous hydration; believing Turia to be the most critical, she attempted to get an IV drip into her first. But by then Turia's burns had caused her body to swell up with fluid making it impossible to find a vein. She turned her attention to Kate and success-fully got a drip into her.

Hydrating Turia was problematical. Dr Brahm could only give her small quantities of water to sip (which the others had done while waiting for help); the doctor was concerned about giving Turia too much water orally because of the risk of aspiration if she needed intubation in hospital. She gave some general pain medication orally; she did not carry stronger drugs, such as morphine or ketamine, because their availability is restricted in Australia and not normally carried by doctors for sporting events.

However, by then the pain issue was moot as the burns were deep enough to have burnt off both women's nerve endings anyway; what was of more concern was the possible irreparable damage to internal organs without urgent specialist medical attention.

It was also too late for any effective cooling: on both Turia and Kate the burns areas were too large and too deep; in fact to have had any effect, cooling would need to have been started at least two hours earlier. While everyone had attempted to keep Turia's and Kate's burns cool, the small amount of water available had had limited effect. Dr Brahm tried to cover Turia with a space blanket but Turia could not stand anything against her skin.

Dr Brahm, as a medical professional, was also aware that Turia and Kate needed life-saving escharotomies – surgical incisions to release the rigid and inelastic burnt skin to help circulation to limbs. This procedure would have to be done in a sterile environment. If it hadn't been obvious before this, urgent evacuation was imperative otherwise these young women would die.

Soon after, two volunteers arrived at the bottom of the cliff in a large four-wheel drive vehicle; they had come from checkpoint three and had driven through the burnt-out territory carrying containers of water and a camp mattress, which they started to haul up the cliff. Shaun made one trip down to help bring up some water and collapsed exhausted when he returned. By then there was an increasing number of people on the ridge. Sometime earlier, Ron Rutherford, seeing the activity there, had also made his way up the cliff with some water, leaving Mary to wait for the rescue he felt sure must be coming.

With the arrival of the mattress, additional thought was given to getting Turia and Kate down the cliff if the helicopter couldn't lift them off. Rod good-naturedly offered to be the test dummy when the men tried to make a stretcher-cum-lifting device out of the mattress and odd bits from their backpacks. Because Shaun, Trent, Wade and Brad had all been trained in underground mine rescue, they figured they could carry the injured young women down on a makeshift stretcher if they had to. But with the risk of further injury if they fell off, the idea was discarded as being too dangerous.

By now everyone on the ridge knew ambulance medics were on the way and the second helicopter was coming from Kununurra.

The ridge had become crowded and it was decided to take Michael and Martin downhill and set up an evacuation point near Mary, where they could wait for transport out.

Nathan Summers, who was also on the ridge with Nathan Tomlinson, knew Paul was an experienced pilot and that if he thought it possible he might try to attempt the high-risk one-skid landing to lift the girls off. He explained to everyone on the ridge what Paul might do and the need to clear away any nearby trees. Those who were able to then set about removing small trees and loose rocks from the area.

•••

Once Sarel's ambulance team reached the burnt-out part of the course, there were no more pink ribbons to guide them to the incident site and they were not sure which way to go. As none of them knew the course, they bumped along blindly when out of the blue, John Storey appeared above them in his gyrocopter; he had heard about the injured competitors over his radio and flown across to see if he there was anything he could do, even though he couldn't land. As he flew over the burnt-out valley John saw the two ambulance vehicles and realised they could do with some guidance: he then circled very low, indicating for them to follow him.

They drove through the rough and blackened landscape until they came across a big four-wheel drive at the bottom of the cliff and a group of people, one of whom was Mary Gadams; they pointed up the cliff of the gorge, where Sarel saw another group of people halfway up. Two ambulance volunteers stayed to give assistance to Mary. Sarel, Dr Waite and one volunteer medic set off to the ridge with medical supplies.

On their way up they encountered Trent, Wade and Shaun assisting Michael and Martin down. Sarel noted that Michael had bleeding legs and Martin was bleeding from the head; he introduced himself as a paramedic. Shaun, recognising the South African accent, spoke to him briefly in Afrikaans, expressing relief that at last someone was there to help. Sarel was then waved on up: 'We're alright – they need you up there.'

When Sarel arrived, Dr Brahm told him she had been unsuccessful in getting an IV line into Turia. Sarel, who had brought additional IV fluid, also tried but had no success either.[2] He administered intra-nasal analgesia to both women, who remained calm but whom he knew must be in shock, if not in pain. His assessment was that even though both had extensive full thickness burns whereby pain was unlikely to be felt due to the destruction of their nerve endings, pain would be severe in any possible areas of second-degree burns where nerve endings would still be receptive to pain.

When ambulance volunteer Bonny arrived on the ridge, soon after Sarel, she surveyed the scene and went to assist him with Turia. She looked at Turia but didn't recognise her friend.

'Hi, Bonny. It's me, Turia.'

Bonny looked more closely; horrified at what she saw, she started to cry. It was then Turia knew things must be serious. Although she was quite numb with shock, she'd looked at her hands and noted only that her fingers looked slightly swollen. The inner Turia was saying, 'It's just a little burn. I'll be back at work on Monday.'

Paul and Bryn arrived at the location and flew over the vast burnt-out area at 4.50 pm. They spotted Summers' helicopter in a small unburnt clearing, saw several other vehicles, and located the group on the ridge with their silver space blankets spread out. As they flew nearer they saw that a small area had been cleared and that Summers was positioned to help guide them in from the ground if they decided to attempt a one-skid landing.

'Shall we give it a go?' Paul asked.

'Worth a try,' Bryn answered.

As Paul set up the approach, he instructed Summers that only two people could be lifted off at a time; this was due to weight issues for the manoeuvre. Those two would then have to be off-loaded in the nearest clearing while Paul came back for two more, after which he would retrieve the first two.

Dr Brahm elected to go first with Kate, as she appeared to be the less injured and more able to cope with two moves in and out of the helicopter; Sarel would go second with Turia.

Bryn verbally guided Paul in on the first approach while Summers knelt on the edge of the cliff controlling things on the ground. Once Paul had the right skid of the helicopter fully on the edge of the cliff, he hovered while Summers held the door open and Dr Brahm and others helped Kate get on board.

Paul flew to the nearest available unburnt patch where he could land, about a kilometre away, and unloaded Dr Brahm and Kate. Bryn then climbed into the rear of the cabin, where he would be in a position to guide Paul in more effectively for the second approach.

Nathan Summers was no longer on the ridge to assist with the second pick-up as he was already making his way down into the valley to guide Michael, Martin, Mary Gadams – and those helping them – to his helicopter so he could fly them out to hospital.

The following is the patter between Paul and Bryn during what turned out to be the most extraordinary rescue of Turia:

On approach:

Bryn: Cabin secure, clear for doors open.
Paul: Clear doors open. [Rear door is opened for better visibility.]
Bryn: Area is clear. Patient in same position, caution loose objects again. [Potential for loose flying objects.]

On landing:

Bryn: Main tail and rotors clear; move right 2 metres.
Paul: Roger.
Bryn: Two, one, hold. [Paul positioned the helicopter directly above the cliff ledge.] Mains clear of the slope but it's close. Tails clear over the edge; right skid above cliff four feet – three, two, one, toes on; heels on hold! Position.

Paul had landed his right skid on the ledge, with sloping ground to the rear, and balanced the helicopter precariously for what seemed an eternity to him, although in reality was just minutes; things were slightly tense.

Paul: Where are they?
Bryn: They're just getting up.

Bryn signalled for Sarel and those helping Turia to limp to the helicopter to hurry up: the delay – agonising for Paul – was because Turia's feet had swollen up enormously, and those on the ground were trying to get her shoes off before walking her to the hovering chopper.

Bryn: Patient approaching from the right rear, clear of the main rotors.

As Rod Rutherford strained to hold the door open, Bryn reached out to help Turia into the helicopter, something he found very difficult as her burns were so extensive – her epidermis (outer layer of skin) was completely burnt and flaking off, revealing her second layer of skin (the dermis) with its white, leathery charred appearance. This meant it wasn't possible for him to just grab her arms and pull her in.

Loading and departure:

Bryn: Patient at the skids; coming on board; moving
across the cabin; medic at the skids; coming on
board; in his seat.

These movements had to be done slowly as they altered
the weight and balance of the helicopter, which Paul had
to correct with the controls. At the same time, the spinning
rotors were kicking up ash and dust into the faces of those
assisting on the ground.

Bryn: Doors closed; seat belts coming on . . . people are
clear to move away.
Paul: Roger.[3]

Paul – adrenalin still pumping but relieved to be safely
away – then flew back down to pick up Kate and Dr Brahm.
Once they were on board, Turia sat opposite Sarel and Kate
sat opposite Dr Brahm. Sarel administered more pain relief.
And they headed for Kununurra.

During the return flight, Bryn made several calls, one
of which was to ask for an ambulance to meet them at the
purpose-built ambulance shed at the Heliwork base. When
he called the hospital and explained the critical injuries of
the two passengers to the emergency nurse, the immediate
change in the tone of her voice told him that she understood the gravity of the situation.

Two of the three Kununurra ambulances were still on
their way back with other competitors. When the remaining
ambulance was not waiting at the airport as expected, Paul,
Bryn and Sarel discussed what to do next. The desperate
condition of Turia and Kate meant waiting for an ambulance at the airport wasn't an option.

Paul circled the Kununurra township several times, looking for somewhere to land, ruling out various parks due to trees or overhead power lines; eventually he decided on a small grassed area in front of Argyle House (which also happened to be the office of Turia's employer), opposite the hospital.

Again Bryn acted as Paul's extra eyes as he made the difficult descent onto the pocket-sized patch; some locals, seeing the helicopter approach, parked cars across the entrance to the street to block traffic. Paul jumped out of the helicopter to assist Turia off and it was the first time he had seen the extent of her burns. He was shocked to find that there was literally no unburnt skin for him to hold on to her. Doctors and nurses came running across the road with gurneys to help Sarel and Dr Brahm get Turia and Kate into Emergency.

It was 5.30 pm, nearly four hours after the fateful six had been caught in the fire.

As she was rushed across the road, Turia kept pleading for someone to call Michael. The last thing she said before they wheeled her into the operating theatre was, 'Can somebody please call my boyfriend.'

Martin, Michael and Mary had been assisted onto Nathan's helicopter and flown to the Kununurra heliport, where they were conveyed by ambulance to the Kununurra Hospital. The others at the site were driven out in the RacingthePlanet and ambulance vehicles.

Competitors continued to race between checkpoints three and six, with one person actually finishing the race at 7 pm. The race was officially called off at 5 pm.

NINE

THE BAD NEWS

MICHAEL HAD SLEPT THROUGH TURIA'S PHONE CALLS THAT morning and when he woke he saw he had three missed calls and two voice messages:

'Oh sweets, pick up the phone; I want to talk to you before the race.'

'I'm about to go into race; please pick up the phone, I want to talk to you.'

Michael detected crankiness in her voice. He called her mobile but it rang out; he checked the time and realised the race must have started and she was probably out of mobile range. He sent her a text message hoping it would be the first thing she read when she picked up her mobile after the race:

'Can't believe you have finished such a huge race. Congratulations.'

He caught his flight to Darwin, arriving later that day. After checking in at the nearby airport hotel he had a swim in the pool. He had dinner in the restaurant and watched a bit of TV in the lounge with some other young men; he saw a news item about a house fire in which an elderly woman died.

'That'd be a fucked way to go, wouldn't it?' he commented to one of the guys. Surprisingly, there was no news about the fire in the Kimberley. After that he went to bed.

At about 11 pm Michael's phone rang. He thought it might be Turia but when he looked at the screen, it was a number he didn't recognise.

'Am I speaking to Michael?' It was an American voice.

'Yes.'

'This is Dr Brandee Waite; I'm the medical doctor for RacingthePlanet.' Michael's heart sank. Turia must have been in some sort of accident.

'I'm afraid Turia has been in a fire and she has burns to more than sixty per cent of her body. She is currently intubated at Kununurra Hospital.'

Intubated? Fire? Michael was confused. He'd just woken up and here was some woman with an American accent telling him Turia had been in a fire.

'What do you mean; is this some kind of joke?' he asked.

'No, I'm afraid it's not. This is very serious. Turia is in hospital.'

'What happened?'

'We're not sure. There was a fire in the gorge and some people got trapped.'

Michael, suddenly awake, felt a shiver up his spine. What on earth was going on? How could someone get trapped in a fire in a gorge – wasn't it supposed to be rocky with water?

'Where are her burns?'

'Legs, arms, hands and feet,' Dr Waite told him.

At the mention of 'hands and feet', Michael asked if there was any chance of amputations. Dr Waite replied that her hands were not looking good. He couldn't speak. How was it possible to get such terrible news from a stranger at 11 o'clock at night?

'What happens next?' he finally asked.

Dr Waite explained that she was critically ill but stable. She would be in Kununurra Hospital for about another hour and then she was going to be medivaced to the Burns Unit at Royal Perth Hospital.

'How did she get out?' he suddenly thought to ask.

Dr Waite explained there was an evacuation with a helicopter.

'How did she get to the helicopter – did she walk? Were you there?'

'Yes, I was there and Turia walked to the helicopter.'

'Was she screaming in pain?'

'No, she was quite calm and she got into the helicopter with some assistance.'

She could walk! That put Michael's mind at ease a bit.

The doctor asked if Michael knew Genji, Turia's brother.

'Yes. I'll call him.'

'No. I will call him.'

Michael's first instinct was to tell her 'no' *he* wanted to call; Genji was *his* mate and she didn't even know him. But he let it go. Before hanging up, Dr Waite gave Michael her mobile number and told him he could call her any time.

Michael was in shock but he didn't cry. Not then. He was still processing the information. Next he sprang into action and called his father, Gary. His father sounded sleepy when he picked up the phone. It was about 1.30 am on the east coast. Michael told him what had happened.

'But the main thing is – she's alive.' He told his shocked father to book tickets for himself and Célestine to Perth and he'd meet them at the Perth Hospital. Next, he grabbed his luggage, which included three big surfboards, and lugged everything down to the front desk to check out. He requested the hotel's twenty-four-hour transport service to the airport.

The hotel's airport bus seemed to take forever to arrive. Michael approached the desk clerk and explained the urgent emergency situation. Normally placid by nature, Michael thought this man remained too calm to have understood the full gravity of the situation; he wanted to scream, 'My girl might be dying, don't you get it?' He just wanted to get to Perth; everything had to happen immediately.

When Michael got to the airport, things were very quiet. Of course it was the early hours of the morning, with few flights going anywhere, but he was pleased to find someone at the Qantas desk. Michael told the young woman that he had to get to Perth as soon as possible. She told them there was actually a flight to Perth about to leave on the tarmac, and there wasn't another one until much later in the day. He begged to be on it but it wasn't possible, the flight was closed; he was told the quickest way to get to Perth was to fly to Sydney and then catch a flight across to Perth. With the time difference, he would then arrive in Perth at about 10 am.

He sat down to wait for the Sydney flight and rang Genji.

On the flight to Sydney, Michael tried to concentrate on the positive. She was alive; she was a tough girl and would pull through. And she'd walked to the helicopter. That was something.

Friday 2 September was a beautiful spring day in Lake Burrill. Célestine had sent Turia an SMS in the morning to wish her well in the big race. At 3 pm (1 pm in Western Australia) Célestine was bringing in clothes off the line and as she walked into the house, her eye was caught by a photo of Turia on the dresser by the door. Turia was in her graduation gown posing by a tree in the university grounds; she was looking happy and proud and the sun streaming through the open door seemed to cast a glow over her. It almost looked as if she was surrounded by fire.

That evening Célestine was restless. As a writer she often worked late. John had gone to bed early as he had his usual 5 am start the next morning. At 11 pm she was working on a part of a story where a daughter is crying out to her mother for help and she couldn't get Turia out of her mind. She tried calling her but it went to message bank. Célestine couldn't get rid of the pang in her heart; she felt something had happened to her girl. She talked herself out of calling Michael and didn't wake John; instead she gave herself a talking to: *Come on; she's just tired after running this big race*; she willed herself to believe it.

When the phone rang at 12.05 am it was Genji. This in itself was not unusual; Genji often rang his mother in the middle of the night to 'have a chat' and tell her he loved her. Célestine weighed up whether or not to answer. Mother love won.

'Mum, I'm afraid I have some bad news. Turia was caught in a fire during the marathon today . . .'

'What?' Célestine listened, heart pounding, while Genji told her he didn't know anything else except it was serious and that he and his new wife, Angela, and Michael's father, Gary, were flying to Perth on the first flight out in the morning. Michael was in Darwin and flying back to Sydney and would meet them at Sydney Airport and they would all fly over together.

'Pack your bags, Mum. Gary will pick you up at four o'clock.'

Her daughter had been crying out to her after all. Pack your bags.

She woke John, distraught, but couldn't tell him anything as she didn't know anything and he sat with her quietly on the deck as she sat, numb with shock, staring out at the shimmering lake. Eventually she woke Turia's brothers to tell them. Toriki, who was twelve, started crying distractedly. Heimanu, two years older, received the news more calmly. 'Wake me when you have more news,' he told his mother and went back to bed.

Célestine set about packing; what to take? Would it be cold in Perth? She had no idea how long she might be there. For some reason she felt she had to take Turia's Cambodian ChildCare cycle ride T-shirt. It seemed important but she couldn't find it at first. But she found a small statue of the Virgin Mary and put it in her bag. She really had no idea what she was going to do with it but visualised getting some holy water to throw over it – and then all would be alright. Finally she found the T-shirt and stuffed that in her bag too; maybe it would give Turia some healing energy.

Gary picked her up and, although Célestine didn't know him well, he was a calming influence on the long drive from the South Coast to Sydney Airport. Plus she gleaned some more information about Turia's rescue from what Michael had told Gary, which she found optimistic. He told her Turia had walked to the helicopter and her heart leapt with hope. *She's alright*, she thought; *something's happened and she's a brave hero – that's typical of Turia*; maybe she would get an award for it.

Genji and Angela met them at the airport. Michael's flight arrived shortly after and he went straight to comfort the obviously distressed Célestine. 'Don't worry; the doctors are looking after her.'

He switched on his mobile and saw he had an SMS from Royal Darwin Hospital; he called and found himself speaking with an intensive care consultant at the hospital's National Critical Care and Trauma Response Centre (NCCTRC), who told him Turia had been transferred there. Her condition had become too unstable for the long flight from Kununurra to Perth. She was now stable and had been intubated to help her breathe; they were taking her to surgery for debridement; that is, to surgically remove some of the burnt skin.

Michael asked if Turia would lose her hands. The doctor was non-committal; it wasn't a yes and it wasn't a no. Michael found some comfort from this although he was left in no doubt that Turia's situation was serious.

They all hastily rebooked to go to Darwin but as they were about to board their flight Michael received another call from the hospital advising him they were planning to evacuate Turia to the Intensive Care Unit of the Burns Unit at Sydney's Concord Hospital; Turia would probably remain in Darwin for an hour or two after they arrived and it was up to him if he still wanted to come to Darwin. The Care Flight was coming from Sydney to get her and the evacuation crew were being prepared; once the Care Flight was in Darwin, and providing Turia remained stable, she would be flown to Sydney.

The decision was quickly made; everyone was going to Darwin. They wanted to be there in case the worst happened – that she might not make it. So a couple of hours later, Michael was on the plane back to Darwin, this time accompanied by his father, Célestine, Genji and Angela. British-born Angela, new in this family, suddenly found herself in the middle of a family crisis. She hated flying but she sat quietly, supportively holding Genji's hand.

No one had any idea why the decision had been made to transfer Turia to Sydney instead of Perth. Only later they found out that there are few specialist burns units in Australia; when multiple burns cases are involved simultaneously, the receiving hospital will, where possible, distribute patients between the units to maximise individual care. Kate, who was also transferred to Royal Darwin Hospital, was medivaced to the Alfred Hospital in Melbourne and Michael and Martin were transferred to Royal Perth Hospital.

At 6.30 am on Saturday morning, 3 September, Michael Pitt received an SMS on his laptop. He and his wife, Karen, had just arrived back from their sailing holiday around the Greek Islands and were staying with Karen's parents in Sydney; Michael's mobile wasn't working. The message was from Genji:

'Turia is in hospital in Darwin in critical condition. She has burns to 60% of her body.'

Michael didn't believe it; this must be one of Genji's old Army mates playing a sick joke. Then he knew it couldn't possibly be a joke – no one would be sick enough to joke like that. Michael borrowed Karen's mobile and rang Genji, who was about to board the flight to Darwin. Michael heard the distress in Genji's voice.

'Dad she's really bad. They don't know if she's going to make it. Are you coming up?'

'I'm on the next flight out.' He immediately bought a ticket online and Karen drove him to the airport.

He bought a new mobile phone at the airport and in a state of shock, blabbered on to the young salesman, hardly knowing what he was saying. Michael didn't know if his daughter was dead or alive. He inserted the SIM chip into his new phone and rang Darwin Hospital. He was put through to the NCCTRC.

A member of the trauma team outlined what had happened – the race, the fire, the rescue, the emergency flight to Darwin. She was in an induced coma. They had pumped her body full of fluids. The hospital in Kununurra had done escharotomies on her arms and legs to release the tight burnt skin and help circulation. Later in the day they planned to take her back to theatre to extend her escharotomies to help improve blood flow to her extremities, which had been further compromised due to the intravenous flooding of fluids.

'I can't tell you if she will live or die but it is very serious,' he was told.

As Michael Pitt sat through the four-hour flight to Darwin, all he could think was: 'Am I going to see my daughter; or am I going to pick up her body?' They were confronting thoughts.

The National Critical Care and Trauma Response Centre at Royal Darwin Hospital has extensive experience in dealing with serious burns. It was set up by the Federal Government in 2005 in the aftermath of the 2002 Bali bombings, when Darwin Hospital became the receiving hospital for the many burns cases. It also received burns victims from the 2005 Bali bombing and treated those from the refugee boat explosion on Ashmore Reef off the Northern Territory in 2007.

Dr Gabriele Weidmann, the intensive-care consultant at the centre, had just started her shift on the morning of 3 September when she was briefed about Turia and Kate. It was a weekend of particular mayhem in intensive care, there were many very sick patients, but everyone was talking about Turia and Kate – what had happened and the difficult evacuation from the Kimberley. Dr Weidmann, a German critical-care specialist with a wide experience in horrific injuries, was told that Turia had sixty to seventy per cent full-thickness burns. Turia and Kate were currently in theatre undergoing debridement.

Dr Weidmann sprang into action; there were calls to be made – families to keep informed and arrangements for transfers. She had to find the Director of Plastic and Reconstructive Surgery, Mr Shiby Ninin, who was attending a conference, fortunately nearby. So busy were they that she paged an off-duty colleague, general surgeon, Dr Steven Hudson, to come in and help out for a few hours but the page went unanswered.

Later in the morning Michael, Gary, Genji, Angela and Célestine arrived at Darwin Airport, where Gary rented a Tarago van, and they made their way to the hospital. On arrival they were escorted to the family room in the Trauma Response Centre.

It was here they met Gabby Weidmann and Belinda Nolan, Turia's bedside nurse. The two medical professionals instantly recognised strong family support behind the anxiety. Dr Weidmann pulled no punches, telling them the outlook was grim, that Turia could die at any minute, and she gave them the reasons why. Célestine broke down. Before this they had dealt with the information through phone conversations, which somehow had made it more remote. Now it was real.

The family wanted to know how she looked. Célestine showed Belinda the photo of Turia in her graduation gown and cap and Belinda knew that was not the Turia they would see lying in ICU. She put her arm around Célestine as she explained Turia was very swollen, especially her face, and looked a bit like the Michelin Man; she was deeply sedated, had a breathing tube in and was attached to a ventilator. Belinda told them it would look very scary as there was a lot going on around Turia and that most of her body was covered in dressings.

The swelling, it was explained, resulted from the body's initial reaction to a burns injury of this magnitude; it immediately starts releasing fluid into the damaged tissue. The fluid is drawn from the circulatory system, which contains the red blood cells, and from the fluid contained in the muscles. This causes profound changes in the body; one of them is oedema – where the body swells up and the blood inside the blood vessels becomes very thick. This is what had happened to Turia while she waited to be rescued and what made it impossible to get an IV drip into her.

The initial treatment was to flood her body with fluid to replace the fluid lost from her organs and keep her bloodstream working. In Turia's case, the situation was exacerbated because she was already dehydrated at the time she was burnt.

Dr Weidmann made them all coffee, apologising for the quality – hospital blend after all – and asking who took milk, sugar. Célestine thought, 'This can't be right, she's the doctor', and offered to take over the coffee-making. Gabby Weidmann waved her off. It was her job to give these people the bad news and she fully understood the shock they were all in; making coffee was the least she could do besides offering comfort.

Next she explained what the escharatomies were for; Turia would need these before her transfer to Sydney. However, she would only be allowed to fly if her blood pressure was stable. Dr Weidmann assured them that Turia would be in good hands; the procedure would be performed by the best surgeons available – this was a hospital with highly experienced burns staff.

'Don't worry about the anaesthetist either – he's my husband,' she said, adding. 'He's also Swiss and very precise.'

Michael tried to take in what he was being told. He looked at Dr Weidmann a look that seemed to say: 'Is she really saying what I think she is saying?'

He had never heard Belinda's use of the term 'Michelin Man' before and didn't know what it meant, nevertheless he decided he wouldn't see Turia anyway; if she died, he wanted to remember her as the pretty, smiling Turia in trendy gear, long dark hair flowing as she ran to board the bus in Bomaderry. Not lying in hospital with tubes every- where, unconscious, unresponsive and unrecognisably puffed up.

He recommended that Célestine not see Turia either. Célestine did choose not to see her, but for reasons that were different from Michael's. She did not want to make this the last time she saw her precious daughter. She was determined that Turia would live. Genji also chose not to see her; although a toughened military man, he could not bring himself to see his pretty, vibrant sister like that. And Angela hardly knew her young sister-in-law.

But Gary said he would like to see her. He came out after about five minutes and Michael, waiting outside with Célestine, was alarmed at how solemn his father looked. Gary gave Célestine a big hug and Célestine, sensing he must have seen something bad, returned to the family room. After Célestine was out of earshot, Michael asked Gary how she really was.

'I don't think she's going to make it,' Gary told him with tears in his eyes.

This was too much for Michael; he found a quiet spot well away from everyone else and broke down. *She's dead*, he told himself, still not quite believing it. *How did this happen?* He thought of all the happy times they had shared. How perfect things had been for them.

On the other hand, he reminded himself that his father hadn't been in many hospital situations so maybe he was over-reacting, whereas Michael had seen dead and dying people when he was a police officer. So it might not be as bad as Gary imagined. Michael hung on to that hope.

Later they all headed back to the airport to pick up Michael Pitt. 'Hello, the mother of my children,' he said embracing Célestine. They sat together tearfully in the back of the Tarago holding hands tightly for mutual support as they returned to the hospital to be with their daughter.

At the hospital Michael was introduced to Dr Weidmann, who told him what the others already knew and the prognosis. It was also explained that if he wanted to see his daughter, she was so full of fluid she might be unrecognisable.

Michael wanted to see her regardless and went straight into intensive care, where he looked down at his little girl. Her body was bloated – her face had swollen to twice its normal size, but Michael was surprised; he expected to see a black burnt face; instead she just looked round and pink.

Back in the family room, Michael could see how seriously his son was traumatised. He and Turia were close in age and close as siblings, but Genji had always been Mr Action Man, catching the big waves, taking the risks, joining the Army, becoming a Navy diver.

'How could this happen, Dad? I always thought it would be me that'd end up in hospital from doing something dangerous. Not Turia; she was always so smart; so careful.'

Michael had no answer. Bad things can happen to good people. He could not say why one person was chosen and not another.

Steven Hudson, a New Zealander who was Darwin Hospital's Rural and Trauma Fellow in 2011, was off-duty on the day Turia and Kate were admitted. He came home from the gym early on 3 September to find his pager had gone off, which he thought was odd because he was not on call. He phoned and was told about a couple of patients with severe burns and how Dr Weidmann had been looking for extra people to help; but things were now under control and he wasn't needed. Nevertheless, as Dr Hudson lived near the hospital, he thought he'd go in and see what was happening.

Mr Ninin had his hands full with two such badly burnt patients and was pleased when the young Kiwi surgeon turned up. Performing escharotomies is time-consuming at the best of times: patients have to first be positioned and cleaned with antiseptic fluid. In this case, applying the drapes was in itself a major task, as it involved all four limbs on both patients. After extending the escharotomies, dressings had to be applied and each limb bandaged. With Dr Hudson assisting, two limbs could be done simultaneously, each surgeon working with a scrub nurse and Mr Ninin overseeing Dr Hudson.

The surgeons were worried that the hands and feet of the two young women may have to be amputated later because the blood supply to them had been severely compromised due to the length of time before being treated. The surgery took several hours and it was late evening before the surgical team emerged.

Dr Weidmann informed the waiting group that the surgery had gone well: the extended escharotomies on Turia's arms had helped release the claw-like contractions of her hands, and her blood pressure remained stable so Care Flight was organising her transfer to Sydney.

Michael Hoskin, detecting slightly more optimism in the doctor's voice, asked if Turia would live. Gabby Weidmann looked at this nice-looking young man desperately hoping for better news. She told him that with medical advances, people in Turia's situation did live these days; she would most probably live but it would be a rocky road to recovery, with skin grafting, scarring, multiple operations and ongoing health issues, her rehabilitation would be extensive and long.

'How long – weeks, months?' he asked.

'Years.'

Years! Michael was aghast. But then, years was better than dead, which was forever. They could get their lives back. He had something to hang on to and felt optimistic for the first time in twenty-four hours.

When it was time to leave, Gabby Weidmann accompanied Turia and her family down the long ICU corridor to the lift; downstairs an ambulance and Care Flight doctor waited to transport Turia to the airport for the journey to Sydney. Dr Weidmann has a lasting memory of those few minutes: Turia's father walking alongside the gurney saying, 'We are here, you can do it, stay strong, don't give up', as if cheering her on to pull her through for a marathon. At that moment Dr Weidmann knew she would pull through.

After seeing Turia off, Michael felt emotionally and physically exhausted; he had flown backwards and forwards between Darwin and Sydney three times in thirty-six hours with only two hours sleep before he received the devastating news. He and Gary decided to book into the airport hotel and get a few hours' sleep before flying back to Sydney because Michael knew he wouldn't be able to see Turia immediately anyway.

The others booked the first flight to Sydney at 1 am; unfortunately it went via Brisbane, which meant additional delay. When they got into a taxi to take them to the airport, the cheery driver, having no idea of the ordeal that his passengers were enduring, was playing Stevie's Wonder's happy hit 'Isn't She Lovely' – a song written to celebrate the birth of his daughter.

Célestine, who normally loved music, could not stand the sound of it right then: 'Turn it off.' It would be a long time before she was able to listen to music again.

TEN

INTENSIVE CARE

AT ABOUT MIDDAY ON SATURDAY 3 SEPTEMBER, PROFESSOR David Milliss, head of the Intensive Care Unit at Concord Hospital, received a call from Dr Gabriele Weidmann at Darwin Hospital informing him about a serious burns patient – Turia – and asking if the hospital would accept transfer. Acceptance would have to be approved by either the head of the surgical burns team, Professor Peter Maitz, or his associate, Professor Peter Haertsch.

After discussing the case with Professor Maitz's registrar, Professor Milliss rang Professor Maitz. Although Intensive Care and the Burns Unit are nearly always at capacity, and that day was no exception, no one is turned away even if beds are in short supply and Professor Maitz agreed the hospital should take her. So transfer was accepted with Professor Maitz as Turia's admitting medical officer (AMO).

Turia was admitted to Concord Hospital's ICU at 5.31 am on Sunday 4 September in an induced coma; the principal diagnosis from Darwin Hospital was full thickness burns to sixty-four per cent of her body – face, neck, right scapula (shoulder), upper and lower limbs. The Concord

ICU team were pleased to note that the team in Darwin had ticked all the boxes before transferring her so that although Turia's condition was critical – in other words still life-threatening – her vital signs, such as heart rate and blood pressure, were relatively stable.

During her flight to Sydney Turia's sedation, administered by automated pumps, had been increased to keep her completely still and she arrived sedated, intubated and ventilated. During the day her sedation was slowly decreased to enable her to start breathing for herself.

The immediate issue facing the intensive care team was keeping her alive. While Turia was young and fit and therefore more likely to survive than someone twice her age who might have sustained such a massive amount of burns, her lean athlete's body actually worked against her. She had a body-fat mass of about ten per cent and body fat is helpful in burns victims because it is a thermal insulator.

Without the fat as an insulator the burns go deeper into the tissues, where it is difficult to treat; burnt tissue releases factors called cytokines into the bloodstream to counter the injuries. This action has profound effects on all organ systems: brain metabolism is altered; so is heart rate, liver and kidney function; and the gastrointestinal tract shuts down. The body in crisis mode starts taking blood from other organs and directing it to the two most important organ systems – the brain and the heart – to help it survive.

The average heart rate of a normal person is 60–80 beats per minute (bpm); the average heart rate of a burns' patient can be anywhere between 120 and 150 bpm. The immune system is racing to try to stop infection and, as a result, burns patients need a three-to-four times higher kilojoule intake than normal; in Turia's case, while she may have been fit, she didn't have a lot of kilojoule reserves to draw on.

•••

By now the story of the runners being burnt in a fire in the remote Kimberley region of Western Australia had become international news. Turia's name was out, and the news spread like wildfire among her friends and the Ulladulla community, where she'd grown up and was a popular figure.

Briggs was on a plane, returning to Sydney after a work-related trip to Thailand, when the news hit the headlines; she went straight home to bed without turning on her mobile. Nicola was skiing in Perisher when someone called her with the news; she immediately packed up and caught a plane home. Her calls to Briggs's mobile went to message bank.

When Briggs woke on Sunday morning she found she had twenty missed calls. The first was from Nicola, who knew by then that Turia was going to Concord Hospital. Briggs collected Nicola and they drove straight there. When they arrived at ICU at 8.30 am, Turia had been there for three hours. They were told she might not live and, to their surprise, were allowed to see her. Horrified, they stared at their unconscious friend; her as yet unbandaged face the size of a football, and undressed arms showing the long incisions of her escharotomies. It was an image that neither will ever forget. Tearfully they both talked to her even though they knew she couldn't see or hear them.

A little later, Michael Pitt, Célestine, Genji and Angela arrived and were ushered into the room where the shattered Briggs and Nicola were waiting. The ICU registrar, Dr James Allen, came out to talk to them and told them Turia was stable and they could see her. Michael encouraged Célestine, saying she didn't have to look at Turia, just be in the room; she could even keep her eyes closed. But if

Briggs and Nicola had seen Turia then Célestine knew she had the strength to see her as well.

Célestine, Michael and Genji stood at Turia's bedside; her face was now bandaged and she was wrapped from head to toe. Turia's eyes were swollen shut and Célestine could just see Turia's little teeth peeking out through swollen lips. The sight of her like that rendered Célestine speechless; she wanted to find words that were empowering but they wouldn't come. Instead she broke into a favourite Tahitian hymn:

E te varua maitai, e a pau mai io matou nei, haapii mai te pure, ia au matou te tetei.

(Holy Spirit descend amongst us, teach us to pray so we can praise the Lord.)

Over and over, Célestine sang these words, praying they would seep into her unconscious daughter; that this call to God would summon an invisible force to empower her on the journey ahead. Turia's breathing seemed to deepen.

'Keep singing, Mama,' Michael told Célestine.

Michael spoke to his daughter, telling her that he loved her; he knew she was very strong and she would pull through. Aware that Turia was a worrier, he wanted to put her mind at rest: 'Everyone is here who loves you; your mum is here; your brother is here. Michael is on his way. Your little brothers are at home – John is looking after them so you don't have to worry. You don't have to worry about work. Don't worry about anything. You will pull through.'

He held the railing on the side of her intensive-care bed, repeating the message again and again, figuring that even if she was unconscious, some part of her deep subconscious must be registering the words. Words he would repeat to the unconscious Turia many times over the coming days.

Dr Allen explained that the next step for Turia was another operation – this time to debride her skin further and remove all the dead tissue. She would be assessed by her surgeon the following morning; he asked her father to sign a consent form.

When Michael and Gary arrived at the hospital later that morning, they went straight to ICU, where they met the others before talking to Dr Allen, who outlined what was happening. They were introduced to the two intensive-care nurses on duty. One of the nurses, Sue, explained she would be looking after Turia and doing all her wound dressings while she was in ICU and said Michael would be able to see her soon. Michael felt relieved and reassured that she was in the hands of professionals.

Sue came out a short time later and asked Michael if he would like to see Turia as she was responsive. Michael walked in and was confronted by an image he will never forget: his girl bandaged from head to foot like a mummy. Only the tip of her nose and her swollen-shut eyes and mouth were visible; she had tubes up her nose, in her mouth, in her arms and monitors everywhere. The bed was elevated and both her arms were raised in a sling. She also had a sheet of aluminium foil draped over her. The sight of his beautiful girl like this was almost too much for him to bear. He felt quite numb.

Sue told him he could talk to her; she would be able to hear him. Michael found this hard to believe.

'Turia, Turia. Michael's here,' Sue said loudly. Turia move her head slightly.

Shit, she can hear me, Michael thought.

'Go on, say hello,' Sue encouraged. Michael went over to the bed.

'Hey, Turia, it's Michael.'

Turia rolled her head over towards him and opened her eyes and rolled her head back again. Michael was thrilled – she could hear him! He could see her big beautiful eyes. She could see him.

'Oh, great. She can hear me,' he said to Sue.

'Yes. Tell her again you're here.'

'Turia. It's Michael. I'm here.' Again she rolled her head over, opened her eyes and looked him; once more she rolled her head back. Michael didn't know if she really understood but was happy to have had eye contact. This was his Turia; she was wrapped up but maybe it wasn't as bad as he'd thought.

Sue talked to Michael about the next step of debriding, adding that the surgeons would also remove some unburnt areas of skin, which would go to the laboratory to be processed for grafting.

'What about her fingers?' he asked.

Sue said she would let Turia's surgeon explain that to him.

She told him the next few weeks would be like a roller-coaster ride. It was an expression Michael would hear many times in the coming weeks and each time he thought, *I've heard that once; I understand. I don't need to hear it again.*

He was about to leave the room when Turia started swinging her arms wildly in the slings and he looked at her. Michael's thoughts were again positive, 'She's moving.' He didn't know why she was moving in such an agitated way, but she was moving. As he left, the nurses were trying to settle her down; her sedation was increased and Turia was returned to an induced coma.

Michael joined everyone in the hospital gardens and they sat together, quietly processing the events of the last twenty-four hours. Then Michael Pitt went back to his in-laws' and everyone else went back to Genji and Angela's apartment in North Sydney, where they had a few beers and continued to talk about Turia and tried to gather more information about the fire.

Célestine said she'd cook dinner and went to change her clothes; she found the crumpled ChildCare T-shirt and put it on. The sight of it prompted Briggs to burst into tears, remembering the great time she and Turia had raising money and cycling around Cambodia.

Early next morning, Monday 5 September, Hal Benson turned up at the hospital to see Turia. On Sunday he had flown to Melbourne with Kate's friend Andrew Baker to meet Kate's parents at the hospital when she arrived from Darwin. He had never met Kate's family before but saw how much they seemed to appreciate speaking with someone who had been on the scene and knew what had happened; with this in mind he thought he might be able to help Turia's family. But it was too early and they were not yet at the hospital. He managed to see Turia, bandaged and in a coma. He left a message for her family and contact details with the hospital but they somehow got lost in the paperwork. It was many months before he saw Turia again.

At 7 am Professor Haertsch was in the Burns Unit theatre preparing the list of operations that he and Professor Maitz would undertake that day. After speaking to Dr Allen in ICU, Professor Maitz had gone down to check on Turia. Alarmed, he immediately went back to the theatre.

'Peter, we have to change everything; this girl has to go to theatre now otherwise she will die,' Professor Maitz told his colleague. Changing an operating list is not as easy as it sounds. But the two surgeons took out their pens and worked out what could be rescheduled; getting Turia into that operating theatre as soon as possible was critical. Dead tissue had to be removed to try and break the cascading effect of the infection it caused.

Burnt skin loses its thermal regulation function and to stop Turia losing precious body heat, it was necessary to keep her in temperature-controlled rooms. This included the operating theatre, where the heat had to be turned up; everyone working in the theatre on severe burns cases wears special lightweight clothes to keep them cool, including the surgeons. A heat-exchange catheter was fitted intravenously into Turia via a femoral artery to warm her blood as it circulated, enabling her to undergo surgery earlier than normal.

Specialist burns surgeons Professors Maitz and Haertsch are also plastic surgeons and are accustomed to confronting horrific burns injuries; but the effects some patients have on them make an impression that stays for a long time because they are different. Turia was one such patient: a beautiful young woman whose body was about to change forever. In extreme cases like Turia's, surgeons face the heavy responsibility of knowing that while they can achieve patient survival, it may come at the cost of a much poorer quality of life – with loss of facial appearance, loss of fingers, permanent scarring, stiffness of joints and loss of independence.

Professor Haertsch was working on Turia's hands, with their long thin fingers, and Professor Maitz was addressing her face, trying not to take it all off. They looked at each other across the operating table. Neither had a choice; they were forced by the injury to remove what was damaged.

It was clear from the start that her fingers were going to be an issue. In burns surgery, whatever is burnt must be removed, not just the skin but tissue as well, and there's not much tissue on a slender finger. Once removed what's left is mostly exposed nerve, tendon and bone, which easily dies.

Burns surgeons have a policy of trying to avoid skin-grafting faces because grafts have a tendency to contract and that affects a person's ability to close the mouth. Because facial skin needs elasticity for expression, skin contraction on the face is different to contraction elsewhere on the body. Fortunately, Turia had sustained only second degree burns to her face which meant it could be saved from grafting. And rather mysteriously, Turia's eyes were not damaged, which is very rare when the face sustains serious burns; it was thought that she must have been wearing sunglasses which protected her eyes, but she was not.

The alar cartridges of her nose (the structure that holds up the tip and nostril flares) was burnt off. Her ears were also severely damaged.

Over the next four hours the two surgeons debrided, as conservatively as possible, Turia's face, neck, arms, hands, both legs and feet. Sixty per cent of her body surface was removed and covered with a temporary artificial skin. The artificial skin, called biobrain, is a semi-permeable membrane containing bovine collagen; it is designed to bind to the tissue, giving it time to heal underneath. The burns debrided during this operation were only those that could be accessed with Turia lying on her back; the burns on her back and shoulder would have to be addressed in a separate operation.

Skin from an unburnt area was removed for the laboratory, where it would be put through a mesher that expands it to four times its original size in preparation for skin grafts. Her surgeons planned to start the grafting procedure as soon as Turia was hemodynamically stable; that is, once her blood circulation was functioning better.

ELEVEN

DARK DAYS

AFTER THE OPERATION, MICHAEL, TURIA'S FATHER AND GARY listened while Professor Maitz outlined Turia's prognosis. Experience had taught Professor Maitz not to go into too much detail with friends and family because most of it cannot be digested. Just tell it like it is.

Turia had a life-threatening injury; she had full-thickness burns to sixty per cent of her body; the burnt skin and tissue had been removed and covered with an artificial skin to help it heal before skin-grafting could start. She had survived this procedure but there was a good chance that she might succumb to shock in the next few days because there was no operation more traumatic than the debriding procedure. If she wasn't in a deep coma she would be running around the room screaming with the pain. She was currently stable but this could change in the next ten to twelve hours. She would need many blood transfusions. Inevitably she would get infections and they could kill her.

On the plus side, she was young and fit. Her face could be saved because the burns were not too deep; her eyes were not burnt either; if she lived her face may eventually look normal again. But she would need a new nose; her ears would be disfigured; she was going to lose some of her fingers, starting with the tips – but not her hands; she would lose a lot of weight; she would have extensive scars on her arms and legs. He could fix Turia but it would take time. She would be in hospital for six months and she would walk out of the hospital like an old woman.

Michael Hoskin listened carefully to Professor Maitz, a good-looking man whose confident manner had put him at ease. Michael appreciated his ruthless honesty.

'So you think she *will* walk out then?' he asked.

Professor Maitz paused for about five seconds and then, looking at him directly said: 'Yes, I do.'

'I'll get her through this. I'll be here,' Michael told him.

But Professor Maitz, having heard the same thing many times before from family members and then seen what really happened, didn't believe him. How could a young, fit, good-looking guy take this on? They weren't even married; he didn't believe the relationship could survive.

'Michael, that young bubbling girl doesn't exist any-more,' Professor Maitz impressed upon him. 'The person that will survive this may be the same intelligent person, but she will look and act differently. The physical abilities she had are gone and they won't come back for many years. Maybe ten years; but ten years for a twenty-five-year old is a long time.'

'But she's my girl . . .' Michael looked puzzled, as if astonished that his commitment could be questioned. He loved Turia and to Michael it was simple: the road ahead might be rocky but it was forward and at least he knew the direction they were going in.

As Michael was not able to communicate with Turia, Sue suggested it would be better for him to go home for a few days. So Michael drove home with his father that afternoon.

Three days later Turia was back in the operating theatre critically ill. Some of the areas of artificial skin on her legs, arms and face had become infected; they had to be excised and the areas rebiobrained. At the same time, more skin was taken from the unburnt area on her trunk in preparation for skin grafting. The following day she returned to surgery so Professors Maitz and Haertsch could debride the burnt areas on her back.

Swabs from all areas of Turia's body had been sent to the microbiology department to be cultured so that the bacteria growing on her skin could be identified. An individual's 'bacterial load' can change when they are injured and large open wounds such as Turia sustained give bacteria ample areas to feed on. When the tests results came back, Turia was found to be heavily infected with a rare bacterium, one that was difficult to control; it was not known where she picked it up but it was assumed to have been something she came into contact with while she was waiting for rescue. It was this infection that caused Turia to lose her face: when the second application of biobrain became infected she returned to theatre to again have her face debrided; from this stage it would become necessary to graft her face thus compromising her scars.

By this time Turia had been in ICU for ten days; most of her burnt tissue had been removed and replaced with artificial skin or her own grafted skin. Even with ongoing infections to deal with, the next challenge was to try to get her off the ventilator. According to international protocols, a burns patient who has been intubated for more than two weeks should get a tracheotomy. Because burns patients generally have injured airways from the flames and smoke, continuous intubation can further damage vocal cords.

A ventilator is monitored to see how hard it is working to breathe for the patient. As the lungs become full of fluid and inelastic it is more difficult for them to inflate. Turia's lungs were not damaged by the inhalation of smoke but by the inflammatory response to her infections. She was now too sick for another operation; her kidneys had failed and her surgeons did not want to take her back to theatre until she was more stable. Each day they would say, 'Let's wait another day.' Finally, Professor Haertsch knew he could no longer wait and Turia received a tracheotomy on 23 September – nineteen days after arriving at Concord's ICU.

Professor Maitz was overseas and Professor Haertsch had become increasingly worried about her continued infections using the artificial skin. Turia had a limited area of useable donor sites; properly prepared, donor sites can be reused up to six times; at first reharvesting can be done at about two weeks, with the length of time between each subsequent harvest taking longer. But Turia's wound areas were not healing and there was nothing apart from dressings with which to close the wounds; in a severe case of burn injury dressings will not help in the long run. If she did not get something done soon to kick-start the healing, she would die from the results of the infections.

Professor Maitz was overseas and it was up to Professor Haertsch to find a solution. His thoughts turned to cadaver skin, which is known to have special properties that can be used to stabilise infected states. Due to the poor rate of organ and tissue donation generally in Australia, there has always been a limited amount of skin available for burns victims. The intensive care team contacted Australia's only skin bank,

The Donor Tissue Bank of Victoria (DTBV), in Melbourne. It was advised that all available skin was earmarked to be on standby for a possible terrorist bomb attack in New Zealand during the 2011 Rugby World Cup in September and October. The New Zealand authorities had taken the bomb threat so seriously they had sponsored several specialist burns education courses in the run-up to the Cup.

Not to be deterred, Professor Haertsch pressed on. With the help of the DTBV and his own international contacts, he located a skin bank in California which had some available skin. The same day it was shipped, cryopacked in a special esky-like container to Sydney, arriving on Saturday 24 September. Unfortunately, Australia's Quarantine Service refused to release it to the hospital because the Human Tissue Acts in all Australian states make it illegal to buy or sell human tissue products.

The messages from the Concord Burns Unit to various Quarantine Service officers over the next few hours were very blunt about the urgency of getting the skin: 'You have two options – adhere to the protocol or let her die.' Finally on Sunday, Dr James Allen, Professor Haertsch's registrar, gave Quarantine the bluntest message yet: 'If we don't get it this afternoon, this patient will die.' The skin was released immediately.

On Monday 26 September Turia had the surgery which ultimately saved her life; from this point, the turnaround in her condition was markedly swift compared to the three-week gradual descent to near-death. Professor Haertsch and his team applied the donated skin to forty per cent of her body surface area. By then the affected areas plus the other areas where unburnt skin had been taken for skin grafts meant that her wound surface area was almost one hundred per cent.

•••

After Turia's first operation, Michael had returned to his parents' place feeling more confident. He liked the fact that Professor Maitz had been so candid; he'd laid the cards out and Michael knew what Turia faced. For the next few days he rang the hospital every twelve hours for an update.

When he received the disturbing news about the recurring infections with the artificial skin and the failure of some of the initial skin grafts, Michael immediately went back to Sydney to talk to Turia's surgeons.

It was the first time Michael had met Professor Haertsch. He was told Turia was going to need more operations but first her temperature had to come up as it was too low. Michael understood that they were still deep in rocky-road territory.

Michael did not go home that day. He took up residence in Genji's spare room and so did his father; Gary bought a double bed and stayed during the week to give his son the support he felt he needed for those first few weeks. He went home to spend the weekends with Julie, giving her grim updates on Turia's progress and describing their son's remarkable devotion and determination that the young woman he loved would come through. If anyone doubted Michael's words that he would 'be there' for Turia, they were now about to be proved resoundingly wrong. Michael bought a little blue Hyundai Getz to make it easier for the sixty-minute each way journey across Sydney to Concord Hospital to be with Turia, a journey he made every day for the next five months.

Gary was profoundly moved by Michael's unfailing belief that Turia would make it. The surgeons were heroes, Michael told him; they'd fix up her face. She'd walk out of the hospital; they had a future and they could have a normal life. During those early weeks Gary spent hours with his son, walking and talking, and never once saw him falter.

Michael knew his girlfriend and Célestine knew that her daughter was made of gritty stuff, and they made an unspoken pact to work together as a team to help her recover. After the first three days on Genji's couch waiting for news of Turia, Célestine had returned to John and the boys in Lake Burrill; Turia was still in a deep coma and Célestine knew it was best to look after the boys until she could communicate in some way.

In the meantime both Turia's father and her partner – the two Michaels – kept Célestine informed from Sydney. The news that she would have to have skin grafts to her face and neck following the second lot of infections with the artificial skin was a shock to everyone; but the main thing was that she was alive.

Célestine came back to Sydney after that. She knew Turia would be heavily sedated but Michael Hoskin had said Turia was responding to nursing commands by turning her head or wiggling her toes. Somehow Célestine knew she had to find a way to communicate with her daughter.

By then, Turia had been moved to her own intensive-care room. Célestine arrived with John and Genji. As they gowned up to enter the sterile room Genji, who had already been to see his sister a few times, spoke sternly to his mother:

'Mum you are not to cry. You have to be strong.'

'You think I'm a coconut head! I'm not – I'm a patient warrior,' she told him firmly.

Before she went into the room she looked at her daughter through the little viewing window in the door. It took an extreme effort not to cry but she walked in, aware that Turia would not be able to respond properly but determined to get through to her somehow. She sat on the side of the bed.

'We are going through this journey together; you are not alone. That's all that matters.' She then started massaging Turia's head gently through the bandages with a soft and soothing technique called effleurage that she had learnt in the previous week especially to help Turia. 'Do you like my effleurage, darling?' she asked. Turia nodded her head. Célestine was thrilled. She could communicate!

Célestine stayed in Sydney, sleeping on Genji and Angela's couch. After a few visits to Turia with Genji and Michael she came up with a proactive plan to move her daughter's recovery forward. She'd noticed that, with best of intentions, Genji and Michael were repeating the same words: Genji was saying, 'This is the calm before the storm' and reminding Turia of things they did as kids: 'Remember the time I wanted you to jump off the roof and you wouldn't?' Michael was telling her how much he loved her and what a great future they would have together. Her father was repeating the same positive 'You can do this' message.

'She can hear you and she's not stupid,' she told everyone. 'She will get bored with all that after a while; everyone who visits must read to her.'

Michael was delegated to read Turia poetry; her father, who had returned to Ulladulla but was driving to Sydney at weekends to visit, was told to read her interesting bits of news and articles from scientific magazines; Célestine elected to read Turia's favourite books. Genji didn't want to be told what to do – he would read or say whatever he thought appropriate.

There was a TV and DVD player in her ICU room and they got her some movies to watch – Célestine believed that even if Turia was heavily drugged, it was important to keep her brain active.

But this was before the breakthrough with the donated skin, and Turia was not out of the woods. When she had to have a tracheotomy after three weeks and her grafts were continually becoming infected and her wounds wouldn't heal and her kidneys failed – those were very bleak days. They were again told to prepare for the worst. They were in the realms of last resort; the hospital was importing skin from the United States and waiting its delivery.

Professor Haertsch had given Michael his mobile number and – after the operation to cover the infected areas with the donated skin on the Monday – Michael called him; the operation had gone really well. They were another step up the ladder to where they could say Turia would live.

Of course he knew there would be more operations. But to Michael, every operation was just another one out of the way; another step forward to her living.

Slowly but steadily Turia's body started to respond to the donated skin and fight the infection. She had miraculously turned the corner; the next goal was getting her out of ICU and up to the Burns Unit on the seventh floor. The tracheotomy stayed in for several weeks and Turia was unable to speak. She was drugged and not very responsive. Michael would talk to her and she would nod; she could move her head or feet on command but her eyes mostly stayed shut. At first her eyes would be closed and he didn't know if she was asleep; he would ask her to wiggle her big toe if she could hear him and when she did he was stoked – she could hear him. As the days went by she began to lift her foot up – that was real progress.

While Turia had been gravely ill during those first weeks, it was decided visitors would be restricted to immediate family, including the Hoskins; Célestine even chose to keep Heimanu and Toriki away. So Briggs was in for a big shock on her first visit since the day of Turia's admission; she arrived to find her friend unresponsive and with a tracheotomy pipe poking from her throat. Briggs promptly fainted. Michael wasn't there but Gary was in the room. He called for a nurse, made sure Briggs was alright and then cuddled Turia, as if to protect her from the drama. Everyone assumed Turia had been unaware of the incident. But as soon as she was able to speak again, she said, 'I can't believe Briggsy fainted.'

On 4 October Turia was finally considered strong enough to be transferred from intensive care to the Burns Unit on the seventh floor. Everyone was very excited. When Michael and Célestine arrived at the hospital and got the news, they high-fived and whooped. They were told she was being prepared for the move and they could see her upstairs in two hours.

But the day Turia was transferred was also the day the bandages came off her face. So the excitement of getting her into the Burns Unit was tinged with the sad reality of seeing for the first time what had happened to her face. It was very confronting for Célestine to see the disfigurement her beautiful daughter would have to live with – the rough and blotchy grafted skin, the loss of her nose, misshapen mouth – so she concentrated on the view from the window. 'Look at this lovely view you have now; you can see trees,' she enthused brightly.

Michael was happy Turia still had her hair and some of her eyebrows. Her mouth was swollen and her nose was diminished. But she was living and he could see her beautiful eyes. Besides, the surgeons had told him they would work with her to make her face look better.

Three days later Turia was due to go back to theatre; Michael sat with her until it was time to go in thinking about the next steps she was about to undergo. Some of the donated skin was to be peeled off and replaced by grafts from her own skin; by then the original donor sites had healed well enough for them to be reused. Professor Haertsch planned to skin-graft her face, neck and arms . . . and, as far as he knew until he reassessed the situation, possibly amputate the fingers on her right hand.

Michael, who had taken over signing the consent forms, had had to sign the form that included amputations but he had not told Turia. He thought, 'Well, if she loses her fingers she's still got her hand.'

It was 7 October, a date Gary Hoskin will never forget. He was sitting in the waiting area of the Burns Unit, a place he'd become quite used to as he had sometimes spent hours there while Michael was with Turia. He saw Peter Haertsch walking along the corridor, head down and looking fairly serious.

'Peter,' Gary called and Professor Haertsch swung around then came over and grasped Gary's hand.

'Can you tell me what's happening with Turia's fingers?' Gary asked.

The surgeon looked at him sadly. 'I'm sorry, but I think I'm going to have to take her hands off.'

'No, you can't,' Gary begged. 'Please no.'

Professor Haertsch, a tall, well-built man with more than thirty years' experience as a plastic surgeon, did not want to remove the hands from the wrists of this young woman, incapacitating her even more. He reached out and squeezed Gary's shoulder reassuringly before walking off briskly. Gary put his head in his own hands and wept.

Turia's hands were saved but the battle to keep all her fingers was lost; that day the fingers on her right hand and one on her left hand were amputated.

When Célestine saw her after the amputation it triggered a very strong emotion. She had lost the big toe on her right foot in a motor-cycle accident when she was eighteen. At the time Célestine's mother had been horrified at this 'disfigurement'; she was told her husband would leave her and no one else would want her. For the next twenty-five years Célestine never showed her bare right foot outside the house; she would bury her foot in the sand at the beach and never wore open-toed shoes.

And what was a big toe when Turia had lost so many lovely fingers? A toe was nothing! Turia must not feel bad about losing fingers and she, Célestine, wasn't going to talk about fingers. She focused on the positive – at least Turia still had a hand. 'You have your hand, darling; you haven't lost your hand. You can still surf and swim.' But Turia, still drugged and fuzzy, lifted her bandaged right stump where her fingers used to be and cried. It fell to the doctors to tell her she had lost her fingers.

Over the next two months Turia underwent several more grafting operations, including procedures to release contractions on her nose and upper lip and the removal of her ring finger on her left hand. All surgical procedures contain risks but for someone as severely injured as Turia with already compromised organs, the dangers of each subsequent surgery and attendant anaesthetic were manifold. Only after about eight weeks was her surgical team confident of her survival.

TWELVE

THE THREE AMIGOS

As Turia started her slow and painful process of rehabilitation, Michael and Célestine determined they would work with her towards the next major milestone – getting her home – even though that was some way off. They began to call themselves 'the three amigos'. Michael and Célestine had established a routine even before Turia was moved to the Burns Unit.

For Célestine, much of that routine revolved around nutrition. Initially, Turia was fed intravenously then via a tube. When Turia was eventually able to eat, everything had to be sucked through a straw. Celestine had long been a devotee of wholesome, nutritious food and her garden was full of fresh vegetables and there was an excellent fish shop five minutes down the road; knowing that good food was a way to build up Turia's strength, she read up on the type of food that would be best for her daughter. There was no way Célestine would have Turia eating hospital food; Michael, who delivered esky-loads of delicious food to Turia's bedside often ended up eating the hospital food instead.

Célestine began splitting her time: she would spend one week in Sydney then one week at home with John and the boys. When she was in Sydney, the boys were looked after by their father or John. Gary Hoskin had gone back home but still travelled up to Sydney every Tuesday on business; he would take Célestine with him, leave her at Genji's and collect her the following week.

During her 'at home' week, she would make nourishing soups from her garden vegetables or from fresh fish; John would help her prepare and freeze the packs of food and she would take them to Genji and Angela's apartment, where their fridge bulged with beautiful food, lovingly prepared. Angela had her new mother-in-law sleeping on her couch every second week and her husband's best friend sleeping in the spare bedroom for five months but Célestine and Michael never heard her or Genji complain.

Célestine's faith kept her going; it was faith in Turia's survival that helped her jump off Genji and Angela's couch at 5.30 each morning to squeeze fresh juices and pack the day's food in an esky. Then she and Michael would climb in the little blue Hyundai for the long drive through the morning traffic to be at the hospital by 7 am.

When Turia was able to eat some solids, Célestine would make small dinners and cut everything into tiny pieces and Michael would reheat them in the Burns Unit kitchen. One of her favourite breakfasts was the pancakes Célestine or Michael would spoon into her mouth in little squares with a dab of maple syrup. 'Mm, yum, Mum,' she'd say. Julie also made tasty dinners cut into small portions, which she would send to Sydney with Gary. But the feeding was a messy business and one that used to distress Célestine until Turia had an operation to release the contractions on her lips.

The days were busy. Turia's dressings had to be changed every day, a painful procedure which could take several hours; because of her Tahitian heritage she was prone to strong contracture and scar formation and this had to be taken into account when managing her scars. Turia also had physiotherapy, occupational therapy and speech therapy. She was fitted with splints on her wrists and hands to stop any unnecessary stretching of her grafts.

Healthy skin has natural pressure which is absent in people who have had full-thickness burns. Without this pressure, the skin will form deep, inflexible scars as it slowly repairs itself over a long period of time. In Turia's case the compression garments needed to be worn twenty-three hours out of every twenty-four in order to be effective. In early November Turia was measured for a set of compression garments for her arms, chest and legs and face; the black face mask was to become her trademark in later public appearances.

Walking is a major part of the healing process for burns patients. After being bedridden for weeks and the numerous operations she had undergone, Turia was very feeble. There was a lot of planning involved to get her back on her feet. From first sitting, she had to move to getting out of bed and walk to the big chair in her room; once in the chair it was difficult for her to get out of it. She was then put into big support boots because her legs were so fragile, and assisted out of her room. The initial challenge was to get to the reception desk, which wasn't far as her room was the first on the ward. Step. Step. Step. Michael found it difficult to watch.

It was extremely confronting for Célestine when she saw Turia painfully step, step, stepping slowly along the corridor with tubes everywhere. She was supported by people either side, a nurse was pushing a wheelchair behind her and the physiotherapist was helping her from the front; Célestine could see each step caused Turia pain. She never cried in front of Turia but tears streamed down her face when she saw her beautiful girl walking like she was one hundred years old.

But small steps lead to bigger steps. On her first attempt she walked to the front desk; within days she was walking halfway along the corridor; then all the way along the corridor. Next she wanted to try the stairs because the corridor was boring. So Michael and Célestine would help her down one flight; it took a supreme effort and she would get tired so they would catch the elevator back up.

Progress was also made on other fronts; Turia decided she wanted to read herself, not just have others read to her, so the occupational therapist rigged up a special book rest which could be wheeled over to the bed. Turia then mastered the art of turning pages. When Célestine arrived and witnessed this for the first time she was thrilled, but Turia said: 'Go away, I'm reading.' Soon Michael was buying her enough books to start her own library.

Célestine also brightened up the room. Because it was in a busy location – a lot of people walked past it each day. Everyone passing could see in through the window in the door and, as there were no curtains around the bed, it wasn't very private. Célestine brought in colourful sarongs to drape over the empty curtain rails. She hung good luck charms and little angel ornaments and family photos. Every day she would put fresh flowers in the room – often frangipani plucked from a tree in the hospital grounds.

Célestine also set up a wardrobe in the room so Turia had different tops to choose from to wear over her dressings. And she painted Turia's toenails to make her feet look happy. Michael brought in some toe rings.

When Turia moved to the Burns Unit it had been decided to continue limiting visitors to family and a couple of close friends: Turia's days were full and she wasn't up to visitors anyway. But in December, her good friend and former Kununurra flatmate Mary flew over to see her. She sat on Turia's bed and the two of them hugged and laughed. Turia was very happy to see her and Michael was delighted to hear Turia laugh again. She had always laughed a lot – a bright, and lovely laugh.

Turia was keen to see her brothers, and the boys were keen to see their big sister too, but Célestine still thought it best to wait before letting them visit; she took letters from them to Turia instead. Turia wanted to reply and to write the letters herself so the inventive occupational therapist fitted her hand with a splint in which a pen could be inserted. But it was heavy going and she became very frustrated so she dictated her letters to Célestine and proofread them before she let her mother take them home.

Dear Heimanu

How have you been? I miss you so much. I remember when you were a little baby and you were so cute. Now you are fifteen and I don't know where the time has gone. You've lost your cuteness but I guess some could say you're a handsome boy.

What's this about you mooning your teacher and friends? I'm glad you got suspended but I can still see the funny side. Me, I'm doing well and my days are full on with visits from the physiotherapists, the speech therapist and the nurses. It's good than I'm busy. The days go fast and Mum and Michael are here. So then I eat Mum's cooking and watch Sea Change. I love you heaps! Can't wait to see you.

Sissy

Turia had defied the survival odds. Once she arrived in the Burns Unit, her progress was testament to some steely determination: her own, foremostly, and that of the other two amigos. The next hurdle was to get Turia strong enough to spend Christmas at Genji and Angela's. Initially Célestine thought it would all be too much for Turia and suggested they set up a special Christmas dinner at the hospital.

'No, Mum, I really want to go out.'

Michael and Célestine had a meeting with the head nurse and explained Turia's rock-solid determination to go out on Christmas Day; how could they achieve this? The nurse listed the issues that Turia would need to face: first, there were three flights of stairs to get to Genji's unit so Turia would have to get stronger at climbing stairs; she would also have to learn how to get in and out of the car; and she would also have to see her face.

In a car, in a Genji's bathroom . . . in fact almost anywhere outside the hospital, there were going to be mirrors, reflections that couldn't be avoided. Celestine wanted to shield Turia from this moment for as long as she could – at least until she felt she was ready to confront the profound change in her appearance.

Seeing her face for the first time since the fire was going to be a major shock. Célestine worried about Turia's reaction. When Turia first started walking along the corridor, Célestine would position herself diplomatically so that Turia could not see her reflection anywhere and she shielded her from mirrors too. Célestine had witnessed Turia's tears through every step of the painful rehabilitation; she wanted her to wait until she was stronger emotionally before that particular hurdle. Turia knew her face had been grafted but she had no idea what she looked like. Whenever she'd ask about her face everyone was careful to be a little non-committal – yes, she looked a bit different but the doctors would fix it up; she'd get a new nose and there would be more operations on her lips. And she still had hair and that was a plus.

Part of the scar treatment was daily massage and Michael and Célestine had both been instructed in the correct massage techniques to use on Turia's arms and face; during Célestine's 'on week' she massaged her daughter's face at night – a special mother–daughter connection, which both found comforting. One day Turia asked to see her face reflected in the window; Michael thought it was okay and was ready to agree but Célestine immediately stood in front of the window.

'Step away from the window, Mum.'

Célestine refused; she did not think the timing was right. 'What do you think, Michael?' she asked.

'I think you should listen to your mum,' he told Turia.

But it was only a matter of time; not long after, Turia asked her father to bring in her iPad and there it was, her face reflected on the screen.

She had cried before since arriving at Concord – with pain, with frustration, with fear. This time she cried inconsolably for an hour. There was nothing Michael and her father could do or say that made her feel better.

Adding to Turia's agony was the discovery that she was vain enough to care; she was disappointed to find that it mattered that her beautiful looks had gone; she never thought she would be that person.

Seeing her face meant that the hardest of the three requirements for getting out for Christmas Day was over; next was some serious stair-climb training. Célestine put a photo of an athlete in the room and told her daughter she had to rebuild herself to become athletic again. Turia had graduated from catching the elevator up after walking one flight down; she was now wearing flat shoes and had mastered the wobbles in them. The aim was to get all the way down seven flights of stairs to the ground floor and back up again.

Turia's efforts on the stairs became a regular sight at the hospital, where the three amigos were already a fixture – the nurses used to joke that Michael and Célestine should move in. Célestine did actually move into the hospital's on-site hostel when she was in Sydney during the weeks before Christmas. She and Michael ramped up their efforts with Célestine doing the morning shift and Michael coming in the afternoon.

After she had mastered the stairs, Turia had a practice go at getting in and out of Michael's small car. It was her first time out of hospital and she wore her black face mask and compression garments, which she was still adjusting to wearing. They went to a local park and had a picnic. It was exhausting but Turia's determined core never wavered. The three amigos had made another step forward.

Dear Toriki,

How are you my crazy little brother? Today Michael bought me some inspirational clothing; for example a shirt with 'Believe you can do it' on the front. So believing I could do it, I tried to walk on uneven ground and I stumbled, failing to catch my steps and I fell but Michael caught me. I was ten centimetres away from the ground. Michael really saved the day but unfortunately he caught me on the sorest part of my chest which resulted in your sister and your Mum yelling at him. But we all had a laugh after it, Mum the most; Mum always laughs the most.

So Christmas! How awesome it's going to be! I can't wait to see Genji and Angela's place, and you two of course. Also pretty keen to see the presents you guys got me (hehehe). The best presents would be a big kiss from my brothers, Toriki and Heimanu.
Love you, infinitely.
Sissy

Christmas Day 2011 arrived and Michael and Célestine helped prepare Turia for her big day 'out'. She had to wear her compression garments but Célestine put her in a colourful long-sleeved top. They arrived at Genji and Angela's; John and the boys were already there waiting for the big arrival. With Michael and Célestine supporting her and John pushing from the rear they helped Turia up the stairs while the others stood at the top cheering her on. When she finally arrived she cried – this time from happiness.

After an hour Michael drove her back to hospital. Another milestone achieved; the next step was to get Turia well enough to go home.

Turia's hands were slow to heal and she had limited movement with them but she continually challenged herself to learn ways to compensate for other movements. Occupational therapy involved working at a variety of activities, such as carrying rings, pegs and fine motor puzzles, all of which were aimed at helping tighten the pincer grip she had with the remaining fingers on her left hand. Frank, her physiotherapist, put her through a regimen of exercises and stretches to strengthen her muscles and movements.

Turia gradually became involved in taking off the dressings on her chest and moisturising the areas she could reach on her legs and torso and as the weeks went by she became more adept at other activities, such as collecting linen and making her bed and moving things around the room. Occupational therapists had made a special long-handled spoon so Turia could feed herself but she found eating even three mouthfuls a challenge and a frustration.

Friday 3 February 2012 was a big day at the Burns Unit. The nursing staff and everyone else who had come to know the gutsy Turia during her five-month stay, and her struggle to survive, popped in to say goodbye and wish her well. Michael and Célestine then helped Turia into the little blue car for the drive from the hospital to a local rehabilitation centre. Her discharge papers included wound and scar management plans, physiotherapy and occupational therapy instructions and a set of compression garments, including three black face masks. She weighed 45 kilograms and her 178-centimetre frame was stooped like an old woman's – exactly as Professor Maitz had warned Michael all those weeks earlier – but she was out!

THIRTEEN

THE ORGANISER'S RESPONSE

OVER THE MONTHS OF TURIA'S FIGHT FOR LIFE IN HOSPITAL, Michael and the Pitt family became increasingly bewildered by what they saw as a completely insensitive response by RacingthePlanet to the tragedy. In a one-page letter addressed to the 'Dear Family of Turia Pitt' and dated 10 September 2011 – one week after the event – Mary Gadams wrote of her 'deep concern' for Turia's injuries. Everyone at RacingthePlanet was 'shocked' that it could have happened and had Turia 'constantly' in their 'thoughts and prayers'.

Given the serious nature of Turia's medical condition, the letter continued, Mary Gadams had asked RtP's medical director for the race, Dr Brandee Waite, to be the channel of communications with the family in case they wished to make contact with RtP. At the same time it had been internally reviewing all the events surrounding the tragedy to make sure it could explain as 'accurately as possible' how Turia came to be injured.

The letter went on to say that contrary to the tone of many of the press reports in Australia, RtP had undertaken 'comprehensive management and risk assessment' planning for the event and put proper risk and emergency procedures in place. The letter stated that in all its discussions in the run-up to the event 'not a single mention was made to us, or warning given, that scattered grass fires which are common in the Kimberley at this time of the year had the potential to flare up and pose a hazard to the event'.

She listed all the precautions they had taken and added that while she was devastated that none of them had stopped the tragedy from happening, 'at least we were able to get help to Turia as soon as possible given the rugged nature of the terrain'.

That comment in particular incensed Michael; how could anyone think four hours was 'as soon as possible'?

The RtP owner said she knew the family's focus would be on Turia's recovery but offered to come to Sydney any time to meet them and discuss what had happened; she gave a contact number. (Kate's family got a similar letter.)

After this Michael received several phone calls from Brandee Waite, who had returned to the United States, asking for updates. After not checking his email for a couple of days he found he had two consecutive emails from Dr Waite informing him that Mary Gadams wanted to do a *60 Minutes* story on the 'amazing recovery effort'.

Michael's return email expressed his extreme disappointment about the way RtP was handling matters: Turia was fighting for her life and they wanted to do a *60 Minutes* story! He said he no longer wanted to hear from Waite because he thought attention was being taken away from Turia. Dr Waite said she understood and would pass on his disappointment to Mary.

The Pitt family were further upset by a Christmas card sent to Turia signed by Mary Gadams and members of the RtP staff; did they really think Turia wanted a cheery

Christmas wish? Even a bunch of flowers would have been more appropriate.

The next communication Michael had from the RtP owner was an email on 12 January 2012, saying that she had heard from Brandee Waite that Turia's family no longer wanted to be contacted, which she thought was entirely understandable given their focus would be on providing support for Turia. She hoped the family had received her letter explaining what happened in the 'tragic accident'. Mary Gadams asked Michael if he and Turia's family would like to meet her to answer any additional questions they might have when she was visiting Australia in two weeks.

Michael responded with an email the following day:

Hi Mary

Ok I'll start by the following, where has RacingthePlanet support been for Turia? Simple question. Turia received a Christmas card from you guys which really rubbed salt into our wounds! I will not vent anger towards you through words as it will not achieve anything. You must be a clever and professional person being the founder of RacingthePlanet. Therefore I would assume you are a reasonable person. However, where has your support, acknowledgement and responsibility been?

Circumstances would have been made easier if you were able to acknowledge what happened and taken some responsibility. I will meet with you if you are going to support Turia in her journey to recovery. However, if you are only going to try and explain to me what you guys did to prevent this from happening I am not interested. I am only presuming you will do this as there has been lack of support for Turia, so I could be wrong.

Turia has lost all fingers on her right hand, her elbows are fused and she cannot touch her face or feed herself. Turia is totally dependent!

If you are willing to help yes let's meet up; if not, enjoy your time in Sydney.

Thanks

Turia's Family and Michael Hoskin

Mary Gadams replied on 13 January saying she 'completely understood' that they didn't want to meet to discuss the event itself but she wanted to get a clearer picture of any concerns they might have and that a meeting would be useful to get a clearer idea of 'the issues would be useful'.

Michael responded on 19 January:

Yes Mary we can meet up. I think it would be best if we all sit down together with the professors looking after Turia at the burns unit on Monday. They can discuss with you Turia's future treatment, insurance costs to cover her bills etc. The RacingthePlanet will have a clear idea of the issues Turia is faced with. Hopefully we can devise a plan on how and what you guys can do to help. Thanks and look forward to Monday.

Mary Gadams' response the same day was to ask if the meeting could be moved to Wednesday morning, as she was actually scheduled to arrive on Tuesday night, but she would be very glad to finally meet Turia's family.

Michael's response same day:

Turia's family are in Sydney on Monday before heading back down the coast. So Monday would be best. We have a room organised at the burns unit where we can all discuss your support for Turia. Now I just want to make one thing clear – that you guys RacingthePlanet are willing to support and help Turia on her road to recovery? Because if you are not willing to help support her the meeting should not take place. So around 1pm?

Mary Gadams' response the next day – 20 January – was that while she could not meet on the basis of Michael's email, she still believed it would be helpful to meet with him, Turia's doctors and her family. To get to Sydney by Monday, she would need to know by Friday to arrange flights.

Michael replied the same day:

It's your call like I said if you are willing to help and support Turia come to the meeting; we will be waiting at the burns unit on Monday at 1pm.

Mary Gadams' reply, still 20 January, was a plea for him to understand that she was not in a position to discuss 'help and support' for Turia at that meeting. But it would be helpful to get a clearer understanding of the 'issues' Turia faced.

Michael, calm by nature but now absolutely furious, wrote:

We ask for help and support. You have failed to do this so far, you fail to help and support us in the future. There will be no meeting. Have given you an idea of how Turia is – dependant!

Mary Gadams responded immediately that she was sorry that they would not be able to meet but perhaps 'sometime in the future.'

Top left: Mum, Dad, me and Genji in 1988 after we moved to Sydney. Dad wanted us to grow up in Australia like he had.
Top right: Dancing the Tahitian way during my first trip back to Tahiti, when I was four. *Bottom left:* I did a bit of modelling during my early years at university. This shot, taken in 2008, is from my portfolio. *Bottom right:* Me surfing in Lombok, Indonesia, in 2010; I was a keen surfer from an early age. I will be again one day.

Above: My two best friends flew to Queenstown, New Zealand, where I was working in the ski-fields, to surprise me for my eighteenth birthday: my Kiwi flatmate, Nicole, me, Nicola Tucker and Kristen Briggs. *Bottom left*: With some of my favourite men: Michael, Toriki, me, Heimanu and Dad. *Bottom right*: With Michael on the day of my graduation – only a week before my accident.

The blackened valley after the fire.

Heliworks WA pilot Paul Cripps making his risky approach to rescue me and Kate. This photo shows how steep the cliff face was.

Paul Cripps's extraordinary feat: no one knows how he managed to keep the right skid of his chopper steady enough to load us on. He did it twice, taking first Kate and then me.

With one of my special surgeons, Professor Peter Haertsch. He organised the donated skin that ultimately saved my life.

With my other special surgeon, Professor Peter Maitz. He was my admitting surgeon at Concord Hospital.

Janine Austen, my wonderful physiotherapist in Ulladulla, working on getting my fingers to bend.

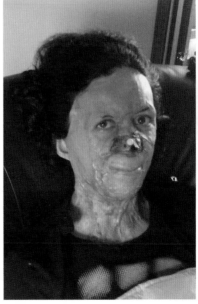

After yet another nose operation in 2012. There are many, many more surgical procedures still to come.

Community support: a montage of photos from the masquerade ball fundraiser held in the Ulladulla Civic Centre and, *centre*, surrounded by our local City2Surf team in Sydney, August 2012.

Michael's parents,
Julie and Gary.

Not about to give up cycling! Here I am on my tricycle, out with
Michael.

The ultramarathon changed all our lives and made us friends forever. Here are four of that fateful six: (second from left) Michael Hull, Hal Benson, me and Kate at a weekend get-together in 2013 with (far left) Andrew Baker, Kate's friend, who was a volunteer at the Kimberley event.

And that was it.

Next Michael received an email from the Racingthe-Planet owner on 9 February apologising for not being able to meet to discuss Turia's injuries but advising him that RacingthePlanet still had Turia's backpack, which had been given to them at the gorge where Turia was injured; where would he like it sent? The email concluded with a message wishing Turia 'a speedy recovery'.

This email was almost the last straw for Michael. If he found the message that Mary Gadams wanted to return Turia's backpack extremely insensitive, the last line – 'a speedy recovery' – was a total punch in the gut. Did these people have no idea at all? Didn't anyone do their homework on severe burns victims and understand the fact that it would take years for Turia to live some sort of a normal life; that she would never, ever be the same again, both psychologically and physically.

Michael heard nothing more from Mary Gadams; that is until the push for a government inquiry into the event gathered momentum in late February 2012. Then, on 28 February, she sent a letter addressed to the 'Dear Pitt Family' regarding what she called the 'extensive media commentary regarding the fire which seriously injured two competitors, Turia Pitt and Kate Sanderson'.

The letter set out in painstaking detail everything RacingthePlanet had done before and during the event to maintain the safety of the competitors – and presumably everyone else involved, such as staff and volunteers, although they weren't mentioned.

However, as the subsequent inquiry found, many of the claims made in this letter – of precautions taken, communications and time lines involved in the rescue – were misleading or just plain wrong.

Michael and the Pitt family did not respond.

RacingthePlanet was to get all the real information of how Turia, Kate and the others sustained their injuries at the inquiry.

FOURTEEN

MY LIFE AFTER

GOING INTO THE HOSPITAL IN KUNUNURRA IS THE LAST THING I remember before waking up semi-conscious in ICU at Concord Hospital. I was heavily drugged and very confused. That day when Michael first saw me in the ICU and spoke to me and I apparently twice turned my face and looked at him – I don't remember that. I remember little about my weeks in ICU. I thought I was living in Tahiti and Michael was not only my partner but also my doctor and we had a child. Every day I'd ask the doctors or nurses what happened because I would forget. Sometimes I would get flashbacks of the fire but I couldn't quite get a grasp of what happened.

When I first woke up with a tracheotomy, my only means of communication was to point and nod and shake my head to commands. It was beyond frustrating; it was hopeless. No one ever really knew what I wanted. My first real means of communicating was when my family eventually brought in a whiteboard and strapped a texta to my hand and I would write words on it. As bad as it was, it was an improvement, and I was able to write things like 'pain', 'drink', 'What happened?' Once, when I was heavily sedated, I asked if I was in a mental institution. Another time I asked if I was in prison.

After the tracheotomy was removed I was able to talk but my voice was a whisper. The first thing I asked for was a sip of Coke – my mouth was as dry as the desert. The Coke tasted so amazing I just kept asking for more and more; I was fantasising about swimming in a pool of Coke and being able to drink as much as I wanted. I then asked for some fresh juice, and more and more of that too. I drank nearly two litres. It was the first time I had consumed liquid by mouth for weeks and my body was not ready for such a large amount of fluid; so of course I spewed.

Being able to talk again meant I was able to tell my family a little of what happened; I told them about the fire and how we were trapped but in the end I didn't speak much about it at all. I don't think my family really understood what had happened to me. But as I was still very frail in hospital, they didn't ask me a lot of questions. I tried to tell Genji but I just got too emotional.

Once I moved into the Burns Unit I began to realise how bad I was and I wanted to die. Michael would come in and say, 'Aren't you happy that you're alive?' And I would think, *Fuck no; I wish I was dead.*

It was hard for me because Michael and my family were all so happy that I was still here but I could not feel this at all. What did I have to live for? My feelings of wanting to die continued for a long time, even after I left hospital. The first time I felt really happy to be alive was when I took part in the Sydney City2Surf with my friends and family in August 2012.

When I had the tracheotomy in, I couldn't speak. It was intensely painful when the nurses rolled me over to change the sheets or my dressings but I couldn't utter a sound to let them know they were hurting me; I could only cry.

I remember once looking at the little cleaner busily mopping the floor and I would have done anything to swap places with him; I was so intensely jealous of his life. Before the fire my life was just great – a great job, a great partner, a great family. I thought about all the things Michael and I used to do in Kununurra – camping, lying in the warm night air looking up at the stars, rock climbing, jumping into waterholes – all sorts of crazy stuff. I cried a lot.

My hands were bandaged for a couple of months; even though I was still heavily sedated and no one had yet told me my fingers were gone, when I lifted my right hand with its bulky dressing where my long fingers once were, I knew deep down there was something wrong. When the doctors told me they had amputated my fingers I cried the tears of overwhelming loss.

The first time I saw my face was terrible. I had been asking and asking about my face and everyone was saying I looked a bit different; that I'd just lost my nose but the doctors would fix it up. When Michael and Mum fed me, the food would fall between my lip and teeth and I didn't know what my lips looked like. I asked Dad to bring my iPad in and that's when I saw my reflection – my whole face had been grafted. It wasn't my face staring back at me. I burst into tears and cried for at least an hour – I could not stop.

I guess I had taken my good looks for granted; I used to think girls who cared about their appearance were vain so I was disappointed with myself for caring so much. I had always identified myself as a sporty, active girl who happened to have good looks as well. And there I was, bedridden with even my looks destroyed. How could I still be me?

Things like surfing and running were totally beyond my reach when I could barely walk 5 metres. After that I avoided looking in mirrors or at anything that might show my reflection. I was also very pissed off because I thought everyone had lied to me when they said it would be fine, that I just looked a bit different. Although obviously it wouldn't be fair to be angry with them because what could they say – 'Yeah, you look pretty fucking ugly'? Of course no one is going to say that.

In hospital I was a skinhead but my hair grew back and that helped. I avoided my reflection for a very long time – perhaps a year – until my psychologist suggested that perhaps it was time I started accepting the new Turia. Now I am comfortable with my appearance as I remind myself that it will only get better.

There were quite a few other confronting hurdles ahead of me, especially during those first few months in hospital. One of them was the first time Mum saw me struggling painfully to walk; I was taking little shuffling steps in big boots along the corridor, supported by all these people, and when Mum saw me she cried. Until then I had never seen Mum cry about what had happened to me; Mum rarely cries – I have only seen her cry a handful of times in my life. That was the first time and *only time* I had seen her cry over what had happened to me. It always makes me emotional to think about that day; if my super-positive mum was crying then – reality set in – things must be pretty dismal.

Seeing my legs for the first time was hard to handle too because I'd always had great legs. The nurse took the dressings off my legs and I remember they stank – even I could smell it. I looked at my legs and they were a bloody mess. I felt repulsed just looking at them; what would other people think if even I found them disgusting? Although my feet weren't burnt, they were still bad – covered in scabs – and my toes were black.

Having my dressings changed every day was really painful and took hours; it wasn't like it could be done once and it would all be over. I'd lie awake at night thinking about how I'd have to go through the whole procedure again the next day. I didn't cope well with the pain; if it had only been once or restricted to a small part of my body I think I would've been fine; but it was *everywhere* and *every day*.

They plied me with different types of painkillers: I would become tolerant to one drug and they would have to change to another one. I sometimes even got the 'green whistle', a drug that ambulance officers used when someone was in acute pain with broken bones or something. I suspect the reason I didn't cope well was because I wasn't in the best mental state and hadn't yet accepted what had happened to me.

I was grateful to the lovely nurses who tried to make it easier for me to bear. My favourite nurse was Penny Gutierrez, a beautiful woman who told me that life can deal us some rotten cards sometimes but it was what you did with the hand you had been dealt that was important. I have always remembered those words and sometimes use it in my public speeches.

I loved my surgeons too; they were always super-confident when talking to me.

A particular hurdle was trying to gain weight. When I was admitted I weighed 63 kilograms. During my five months in hospital I lost a staggering 16 kilograms. All my fat, of which I had little to begin with anyway, was long gone and my body was eating away my muscles. As much as I tried to gain weight, I couldn't; all my food would be consumed by the healing process of my wounds. In the early months I had a nose tube put in that went straight to my stomach, feeding me high-kilojoule liquid food. I hated the nose tube – it hurt every time I twisted my head and every time I swallowed. When finally I could eat solid food, I would eat and eat and eat and I still lost weight.

The love and care Michael and Mum gave me all those months in hospital was inspiring. They never gave up urging me on and it can't have been easy. I remember once the physios were trying to get me to walk up a single stair and Mum and Michael kept coaxing me on saying, 'You can do it' and 'Well done' and I just lost it at both of them. I said to Michael, 'What are you cheering for – your fucking cripple of a girlfriend?' He looked so hurt and I was pleased that I managed to hurt him.

Michael came every single day; Mum came every day for a week every second week. They brought loads of yummy food and books and good luck charms and flowers and family photos and letters from my little brothers and get well messages from everybody and T-shirts with positive slogans.

Michael was always so encouraging, talking about our future together, never failing to comment on the progress I was making or how great I was looking and how beautiful my eyes were.

As for Mum, it didn't matter what it was, she would find something positive to say. She said I was born with a *manu* (big) nose and told me that when I was little I wanted to have a *pupa* (small) nose and now I did. About my fingers she said it was wonderful that I still had my hands and I would learn to do all sorts of things with what fingers I had left. When she brushed my hair she told me what beautiful hair I had. When she painted my toenails she said what pretty toes I had.

When she massaged my feet she reminded me that I had always been into creative visualisation with my running and now I should visualise myself differently – to call on my imagination and visualise doing all the things I used to do. Even running.

We used to play a game just to make ourselves laugh: outside the fire exit of the Burns Unit I would gaze at the cows in the paddock and pretend I was the Queen and talking to all my subjects. Mum would be my lady-in-waiting and Michael would be my suitor.

One of my favourite memories of when I was in hospital was one day when it was raining. Michael was pushing me around in a wheelchair as I was still quite frail and I decided I wanted to feel the rain on my face – it's the sort of thing most of us take for granted. So Michael was persuaded to wheel me outside in the rain and it felt wonderful, like a completely new experience.

At first the thought of what was in front of me was daunting. Michael and Mum would tell me about all the things I would be able to do again in a few years. I would think, *Fuck, a few years!* Every time a patient in the Burns Unit went home, I would think, *When do I go home?* I wanted to run, surf and be back at work again. Instead I had to be content with being able to do the most basic of tasks: trying to get my lips together; trying to touch my face with my hands; getting my shoulder range past 90 degrees; trying to eat with the extendable spoon; trying to sit on the toilet seat. While I was happy when I achieved any of these tasks, the actions were still tinged with despair. I couldn't even walk up a flight of stairs – how would I ever run again, let alone be strong enough to charge into the surf.

I also had a bad anaesthetic experience: the anaesthetist tried to intubate me while I was awake, after which

I was not able to eat for a month. This put me off having operations altogether. So then I would think, *If I can't even handle an operation, how am I going to have all my operations in the future?* It infuriated me more when Mum and Michael said to me 'You'll get through it.' Why wouldn't they just let me die?

I was on a roller-coaster of emotions; sometimes I would use my angry thoughts at the race organisers to push myself even harder. I would think, *Fuck you if you think you can kill me; I'm going to come back bigger than ever.* And there were some days when I would just be overwhelmed by it all and I just wanted to watch TV. I would go from feeling positive and confident that I was going to 'beat' this accident and then I would feel overwhelmed again and hate everyone, including myself.

One thing that helped me to stay positive was to keep busy. Mum and Michael would arrive at the hospital and be there at 7.30 am. After breakfast I would go for a training session with Michael or Genji. Genji was in charge of my 'training' while I was in hospital and later in rehab. He would come in the early morning if he wasn't at work. He bought me some strap-on weights and we got straight into it – squats (well, sort of), shoulder raises and biceps – whatever I could manage with the ossification in my elbows.

When Dad came to visit we did more yoga-type movements.

At 9 am I would have physio. Then I would have a dressing. After lunch I would have speech therapy. Then I'd fall asleep and the physios would wake me up for an afternoon session. Then Mum, Michael and I would walk the seven flights of stairs down and then up again. Then, to help my knees bend, we would have to put the CPM (Continuous Pressing Machine) on my legs for two hours as well as use a special splint to help open my mouth. At the end of the day I would usually be so exhausted that I would be grateful to be left alone to sleep.

Michael initially heard from *60 Minutes* producer Ali Smith after they'd done their first piece on the fire and the rescue – just after it happened. There was no way I could have been involved in that – I wasn't even conscious – but Ali wrote to me and said that if in the future the time was right, would I consider meeting her to do a story with *60 Minutes*? Obviously, the fire had created a lot of media attention and there was a lot of interest in hearing my and Kate's stories.

The first time I tried the mask on, Michael decided to take me outside; I didn't like it and all I could think about was how bloody uncomfortable it was. Gradually I built up the tolerance to spend more and more time in the mask but it took me a couple of months before I started to sleep in it. After that I wore it for 23 hours a day. Since then I have had to get used to being without it and getting used to the new Turia.

By December I felt I was ready to talk to Ali and I got Michael to call her. I told her I was considering doing a story because I wanted to show people that no matter what hurdles you are faced with, you can overcome them. I wanted to inspire others and that was my main motivation. I made it clear that I didn't want to waste my time using the media to vent my anger at the race organisers for failing to properly ensure the safety of their competitors. I didn't want to be part of a sad and angry story.

I invited Ali to come to the Concord Hospital Burns Unit in early December. The plan was that she would meet Michael first so he could explain the extent of my injuries to her before the three of us talked. I had just had surgery on my face and decided to let her see me with my mask off.

This was not the first time I'd been seen without my mask; one day Mum and Michael had wheeled me out into the waiting room and people came over and said things like, 'Oh, my God; what happened to him?' or 'I'll pray for him.' I was a skinny skinhead and they all thought I was a boy. Maybe they also thought Michael was my gay lover.

The meeting with Ali went well and she discussed how she thought they'd present my story; a week later she brought the *60 Minutes* reporter Michael Usher to meet me. We connected straight away, which was good, because from our discussions I knew I was going to have a lot to do with him. The theme of my story was me achieving milestones, filmed in small sequences and presented on several *60 Minutes* programs over the next couple of years.

The first filming was done in that December. I was actually happy to do the filming – it made me feel good about myself and I was also happy that people were interested in my story. I think this interest stems from the circumstances of the fire – an ultramarathon plus the failings of the organisers. I reminded myself all the time that I was 'lucky' – if I had been burnt in a house fire I'm not sure many people would have cared.

I visualised myself getting out of hospital for Christmas Day. Mum tried to talk me into having a family feast at the hospital. No way. I wanted to be at Genji's place, where everyone else in the family was gathering. They didn't understand that what I wanted was a sense of normalcy.

I'd had an operation three weeks before Christmas, and Michael and Mum were both concerned about me pushing myself too hard and thought that perhaps it would be easier for me to stay in hospital. Normal procedure after an operation is bed rest for five days but my legs managed to get blisters so I was on bed rest for another five days. This left me less than two weeks to build up my strength to climb two flights of stairs as well as practise getting in and out of a car.

I'd never even seen where Genji and Angela lived. They had an upstairs flat so I knew I had to practise climbing stairs, and I did. It was hard but each stair was an achievement. The skin over my knees was as hard as a rock so it hurt just to bend them that little bit needed to climb stairs.

The other problem I faced was my balance: at first I would only climb stairs one at a time and only if Michael and Mum were on either side of me.

In the beginning I couldn't climb a single stair without the support of two people and it took about ten minutes just to climb three stairs. I was happy when I was finally able to do this. After practising stairs on a daily basis, I was able to climb a full level by myself. I told Professor Maitz, hoping he would be happy with me, and he said, 'So . . . why not do them all?' I thought, *Fuck you, I will do them all*. I got to Level 5 and then needed to lie down for the rest of the day!

My next goal was to complete the whole seven levels from the Burns Unit to the ground floor and back up again. Every day I pushed myself as hard as I could and to climb one more level – a lot of lying down afterwards was needed. I finally conquered my goal and managed to do all the seven levels in thirty minutes. After that, whenever I wanted to go outside, which was every day, I made myself walk down the stairs to the ground floor and then back up to the seventh floor. In the end I could do that three times a day and had cut my time down to about ten minutes. Today, I always take the stairs anywhere I go; I reckon if you've got legs you should use them!

I loved going to Genji and Angela's on Christmas Day, even though I cried when I first saw everyone. Mum had gone overboard and covered all the mirrors with sarongs, thinking it was best to protect me from seeing myself. By then I was actually starting to think I should be facing up to my appearance, not hiding from it, and I'd even shown my face to Ali from *60 Minutes*. I knew Mum meant well, and we would have to deal with the mirror stuff later.

It was so great to see my younger brothers; Toriki confessed to me, with teary eyes, how happy he was that I was still here.

I was just so happy to be at Genji's. It was a real achievement – very emotional and tiring, but I did it. I knew then – and so did everyone helping me to get better – that I could push myself and get results.

Next I visualised myself walking out of the hospital for good – the Burns Unit was becoming less challenging and I felt I had outgrown it. My doctors agreed. Michael and Mum checked out a rehabilitation place on the north side of Sydney. Michael said it was awful but Mum, looking for a positive angle, told him, 'No, look, there are some beautiful frangipani trees outside; it's going to be alright.' So it was arranged for me to stay there for a few weeks.

The day I left Concord Hospital was an important milestone and also a bit emotional. Everyone I knew in the whole place came to say goodbye and wish me well. *60 Minutes* came along to film the rehab milestone.

Unfortunately, I hated the rehab place. The staff was professional but the facilities were pretty third world. I felt like a fish out of water as most of the people's rehab needs were so different to mine – there were lots of people with brain injuries, like car accident victims and elderly people, who had had strokes or else accidents such as falls. There was only one other burns survivor there whom I unfortunately didn't get to talk to because he had an infection.

Michael was right – it was awful. The showers were disgusting and he worried about me getting infections. So much for Mum's beautiful trees!

My first night I was there I started feeling sick and I felt even worse the next day – I actually thought I was dying. The next day a nurse apologised to me for forgetting to give me some of my pills! It turned out that I was suffering withdrawal symptoms from not having all my drugs. They had explained to me at hospital that although I wasn't in as much pain, I would still need to take painkillers and I would need to wean off them *slowly*.

When Michael and Mum weren't there I was lonely, especially at night. The second week I was there I was allowed out to go to Genji and Angela's for the weekend. I slept next to Michael and cried with happiness. That was what I really needed: to be with the people I loved.

Michael was worried about me in that rehab centre and wanted to get me out. I begged Mum to stay overnight with me once and they found a bed for her; I think staying with me that night made her realise how miserable and depressed I was. Michael and Mum then campaigned for me to go home earlier.

We decided that the best place for me to stay when I left the hospital system was with Michael at his parents' place. Gary and Julie's house was in a quiet cul-de-sac and quite private, which I liked because I got so exhausted and I felt I needed my privacy.

Michael had learnt how to do all my dressing changes at Concord and did them all while I was at rehab and this was the really major thing. Of course, Michael had been caring for me from the beginning – feeding me, giving me my pills, putting my mouth splint in, putting my compression garments on, brushing my teeth . . . everything. I made sure I could do all my toileting before leaving rehab as I thought it was important to maintain some dignity.

Julie organised a local physiotherapist, Janine Austen, to look after me. Michael arranged for another local, Gregg Orphin, an exercise physiologist who did rehabilitation – he knew him through surfing – to work with me. Eventually I had a fantastic local team: my personal trainer, Emily Bingham; my general practitioner, Herbert Chee; the owner of the Xtreme Fitness gym, Lloyd Egan; masseuse, Nicola Parnell; my yoga instructor, Himani; and my psychologist, Jennifer Clarke. So three weeks after I went into rehab, I was out again.

It was exciting to be on my way home. It was a tight fit getting the three amigos and everything else into Michael's little car; we were loaded up with my 'toilet seat' – a raised platform, higher than a toilet – a cushion for me because I got a sore bum from sitting plus all the stuff I had accumulated while I was in hospital – cards, gifts and clothing. The trip was long and slow as we had to stop a few times because I needed to stretch my skin. After even an hour in the car it was so hard just to walk because my skin was as stiff as a board. I was wearing my 'uniform' – my pressure suit and my mask.

FIFTEEN

MORE MILESTONES

WHILE I HAD BEEN REALLY LONGING TO GET HOME, ONCE there it was a little disappointing because I was hit with the reality of not being able to do all the things I used to do – I couldn't surf, I couldn't swim, I couldn't run and I couldn't hang out with my friends. I was in a lot of pain and taking four different kinds of prescription painkillers. Michael used to encourage me to get up and walk around and I'd have a big whinge because it hurt. He also made me go for walks before physio, which I dreaded because I was so stiff. Calcium builds up in the joints of people with severe burns and that makes it difficult to flex our joints. So I couldn't bend my elbow to scratch myself or shower myself. The scar tissue also limited my movements. But I set myself milestones. One was to be able to touch my face with my both hands.

Because I had left rehab early I was initially going to physio each day for an hour and a half. Janine was terrific; she would work with me doing passive, gentle stretching to try to get some movement back so I could gradually start to do a few things unaided. Physio was painful and I had to have a lot of painkillers to get me through a session with Janine.

When I first started going to Janine's I had a lot of open wounds that were slow to heal. When the grafts broke down I'd have to go back to hospital to have them regrafted; I'd stay overnight. I also went back to hospital several times for other procedures on my nose, lips and hands.

The best operation was the one to fix my left hand. The burns had caused my hand to curl over into a fist and it was virtually useless. Professor Maitz advised that we shouldn't do the hand until I could touch my face. They surgically straightened my left hand (it's now permanently fixed at an angle of 30 degrees). I couldn't believe how good it was to have a functional hand; I could open doors, brush my teeth, use my computer better and so on.

As Michael had become my full-time carer, whenever I had dressings, it was his job to change them. When I didn't have dressings, I could hop out of the shower and Michael would put a towel around me and help me get my clothes on. When I had dressings, a shower was inevitably followed by a dressing so I hated getting in that shower. Having the dressings changed was painful and I'd get shitty, and Michael would get upset because he was causing me pain – but he couldn't help it; it was something he had to do. We dealt with it by acknowledging that it would be over when it was finished; that I would continue to heal and one day I would have no dressings at all.

Some of my compression suits were too tight over certain joints. I would only wear them if they were comfortable, and a lot of effort went into getting them right. They were initially too tight over my elbows and wore my skin down until I had two huge wounds. I was so upset as they had only just healed and they had taken a couple of months to heal. Then they were too tight over my knees and made the skin on my knees break down. Everything I have now is fantastic. I wear a short-sleeved compression suit that looks like a short-sleeved wettie, and a special bra with arm sleeves that came from France. Occupational therapists attached to Concord Hospital in Sydney measure and fit me for the garments.

Right now I still can't go in chlorinated water but we were told salt water would be good for healing. The first time I got back in the water was in March, only a few weeks after I came home. Michael and Janine took me to the local saltwater pool; I wore my boardies over tights. Mum turned up, and we all walked down the steps at the shallow end and I walked with their support across the pool from one side to the other (about 5 metres). We did that five times and afterwards I was exhausted. I needed their support because I was still a bit frail and might have toppled over. Being in the water felt terrible; it stung my wounds and it was cold. But I knew it was good for my skin and I knew that my life revolved around the water so I would have to get used to it.

In April 2012, Michael and I flew to Perth so I could give evidence at the Western Australia Government's inquiry into the fire. I was determined to be there but it was an extreme effort and a very emotional time for me as I was still very unwell. Kate was flying over from Melbourne and we arranged to all stay at the same hotel. It was the first time I'd seen Kate since the fire; we cried when saw each other and then compared battle scars. We had not had much contact until then. Hully and Shaun were there too and after giving our evidence we all went out for lunch. I puzzled over what we were celebrating. Were we celebrating the fact that Kate and I were badly burnt? Michael and I left lunch early and I curled up in bed and cried for the rest of the day.

The first *60 Minutes* program went to air the following month and showed a clip of Kate and me walking into the inquiry and we both looked as frail as we were. *60 Minutes* was overwhelmed by the response it got to my story and so was I. Its mailbox was filled and Ali sent me all the personally written letters, sometimes accompanied by pictures drawn by children. I found the experience quite moving. Here are some of the comments from the *60 Minutes*' email:

> We should all take a Leaf out of Turia Pitts book what an amazing individual after everything she has been through she's still shockingly positive and calm about her whole situation, I hope she has a long happy life with her totally devoted partner by her side what a beautiful couple I wish them all the best.
>
> Carmen

> An indescribable journey by an inspirational lady. Thank you dear Turia for sharing your story. It is a story that will be kept in my heart, where it will never be forgotten.
>
> MarkThompson

> Turia Pitt is a true inspiration. With her positive outlook on life, she has everything she needs to succeed in the future. My husband suffered 65% 3rd degree burns 13 years ago and it hasn't stopped him from achieving his dreams. Turia shares his same determination, drive and passion for life. I feel like we were watching our story on screen and just want to pass on our best wishes to Turia and her partner, we have walked in your shoes and there truly is a wonderful future ahead for you . . . although you already know that!
>
> Coreena Musilino

Turia, you are an inspiration to us all. You are a triumph to the human spirit against all the odds. May I wish you all the best in your recovery and with the amazing Michael by your side; you have so much to look forward to. Your drive and ambition will get you wherever you want to go . . . But where are the Racing the Planet race organisers? They appear to claim no responsibility but to not show a scrap of concern for those injured is not only insensitive, it's just plain wrong. Come on Racing the Planet – step up to the plate and help these athletes who are so clearly in need of help.

Natalie, Ulladulla.

The second segment about me went to air in August 2012 and once again the *60 Minutes* mailbox was full of similar comments.

After a while life settled into a routine. Rehabilitation had become a full-time job, and even today still plays a big role in my life. I was up at 7.30 am and breakfast was followed by a protein shake (protein, banana and egg). Then Michael would drag me out of the house for a quick warm-up walk before physio. Even though our walks were usually gentle they would really tire me out. After physio with Janine, I'd go down to Mum's for lunch and a massage. Professional masseuse Nicola Parnell is one of Mum's neighbours and she gave Mum a massage table, which was a great help for us. Sometimes Julie would come down and help as well. Later Nicola took over doing the massage from Mum. In the afternoon Dad would take me to the Xtreme Fitness gym for muscle strengthening. I was very determined to get stronger. Because I couldn't lift weights, Dad organised some wrist splints with hooks to attach the weights to. After the gym I would return home exhausted. At first I used to just zone out in front of the telly but as my energy levels increased I was able to start studying again.

Little by little I started making progress. I learnt things like how to dress myself and to use my pincer grip to undo buttons. Janine suggested kayaking would be good exercise and I bought a pedal kayak so I could propel the kayak with my feet as I couldn't paddle. Janine was the first person to go kayaking with me; we went to Burrill Lake and it was fun. After that I started going with Michael or a friend. I'd loved bike riding enough to enter a triathlon in Kununurra but it was now impossible for me to ride a normal bike. Janine suggested getting an adult trike, which I did, and that enabled Michael and me to go riding together. But I will ride a normal bike again one day.

The biggest challenge was being able to feed myself; I was very thin, and having others feed me was not conducive to weight gain. I had left the hospital weighing 47 kilograms and I still wasn't gaining weight. The occupational therapists in the Burns Unit had made me an extended spoon but I didn't like it; limited mobility in my wrist made it very hard to twist it to my mouth. My aim was to be able to feed myself before the first anniversary of the fire. I found some special cutlery in a local shop that caters for people with disabilities and it was easier to use. I finally managed to get my fork to my mouth in July 2012. I was trying very hard; the fork was wobbly and everyone at the table was looking at me, willing the fork towards my mouth. 'Don't watch me!' I told them crossly. They all tried not to look at my struggle; but when I got it to my mouth everyone at the table was happy.

I was finally able to touch my face with my left hand in September 2012. That was a huge moment and everyone cried, not just me. I am still working on getting my right arm to my face.

A year after I took my first wobbly steps in the ocean pool, I was swimming half a kilometre over arm and breast-stroke. I felt a bit uncoordinated and probably didn't look too graceful but that didn't matter. I can go in the surf with Michael but I don't really enjoy it much yet as I am still a bit weak and the waves knock me around. But I do it because the more I do it the stronger I'll become. I will eventually be able to surf again – I just need my right elbow to be more flexible and I also have to be able use my hands to push myself off the board.

I haven't yet got to the stage with running where I enjoy it; it hurts around the ankles, where it feels quite stiff, and it hurts my knees. I do beach sprints on soft sand and the first time Michael timed me doing 100 metres in 21 seconds I was stoked. I did my first public run (sort of) in Sydney's City2Surf in August 2012 and managed to walk 8 kilometres; *60 Minutes* came along for that. A couple of weeks later Michael and I flew down to Melbourne so I could participate in the Ultra Spirit fun run in the Botanical Gardens, a fundraising event for both Kate and me organised by Samantha Gash, a friend of Kate's who was also a runner in the Kimberley Ultramarathon.

It was quite sad that Kate wasn't able to participate because she was back in hospital, having just had half her foot amputated. Michael and I visited her in hospital but I could only stay for a short time; I think she put on a brave face (like I often do) for our visit, but I could tell she was upset about the foot and everything else. Who wouldn't be?

SIXTEEN

A LIFE BEYOND

THERE ARE SO MANY MORE THINGS I CAN ACHIEVE OVER THE rest of my life. I am very goal driven and wake up every morning with a plan. One of my early plans was to see if there was somewhere in the world that might be able to give me some additional help with my rehabilitation, especially my scars. I found the Ster Centre, a specialised clinic set up by Dr Jean Ster in the pretty town of Lamalou-les-Bains in the south of France. There was a range of medical rehabilitation available there and one dealt with burns injuries.

Professor Maitz thought it would be a really good idea for me to go; he told me the centre was one of the best in the world – offering lots of hydrotherapy, occupational therapy, exercise and mental strengthening. I wrote to the doctor in charge, Dr Nicolas Frasson, explaining my situation, and he wrote to Professor Maitz asking for more information about me. Professor Maitz gave him a detailed description to enable him to take over my treatment while I was there. I booked myself in for six weeks' treatment and Michael and I flew over in mid-March.

It's about a twenty-three-hour flight from Sydney to Paris, not to mention the three-hour drive from Ulladulla to Sydney. Professor Maitz had advised that I would need to go business class because otherwise I would not be able to sit for that long with my burnt bum.

Once in France, we hired a car and drove down; when we were driving into Lamalou-les-Bains, I was so nervous I kept grabbing Michael's hand. 'What if I don't like the clinic? What if they are mean to me? What if no one understands me?' I was kicking myself for travelling across the world to a clinic that I didn't know much about.

Luckily, I discovered that all my worries were unfounded. The clinic was absolutely amazing. I stayed in accommodation on-site during the week. Michael would go off exploring different places to surf and snowboard then come and collect me for the weekends, and we would tour around so I got to see a bit of France, which was fantastic. We went to Versailles, the Alps, the small town of Lodève, and Toulouse; *60 Minutes* came over and filmed us in Paris. They then came down to the clinic to film all the things I would do in a typical day and the different treatments I was undergoing.

The treatment was full-on and each day was hectic. I'd start with a group warm-up and stretching session, after which I went to something called *mechanotherapie*, where I was rigged up in a system of pulleys and left for forty-five minutes – a bit like being drawn and quartered but not as painful. Next I'd have a facial where my face was stretched and massaged, after which I was treated with an LPG machine, a device for treating connective tissue developed by Frenchman Louis-Paul Guitay which sucks up the skin and pushes it between rollers. That was followed by a facial exercise class aimed at improving facial expression. Then

I'd go to *ergotherapie* – a group class designed to improve hand function. My favourite part of the day was a body massage combined with the LPG machine on my body; it was followed by my least favourite part of the day – when I changed into my swimmers and got hosed with high-pressure water. Then I had a chemical-free spa and after getting dressed had hand stretches, followed by twenty minutes of *plateau canadienne* – this was basically a board which immobilises your hand. It's fine for the first ten minutes and then it kills for the second ten. To up the torture levels, they put a splint in my mouth to increase the range with which I can open my mouth and smile. The last treatment of the day was another session of *ergotherapie*. At the end of each day I was bloody exhausted and usually went to sleep around 9 pm.

I experienced improvements quite soon, especially in my flexibility. When Michael picked me up at the weekends he would immediately notice the difference in my skin: reduced redness and an increased suppleness. At the clinic I became friends with an Irish guy called Matthew; the poor guy had worn a sheep costume to a Halloween party and some idiot set him alight. No one else spoke English so it was good to have someone to compare battle scars with.

One of the best things about the clinic was regaining my independence from Michael and my family. It made me understand that there is a piece inside of me that the fire didn't get – that I am still an independent woman; I am still Turia.

The clinic was also good at showing me little ways to improve my self-reliance, such as providing a gadget to help me put my shoes on. Those things were very good for my self-confidence. The clinic made me a whole lot of splints to stretch my hand out and a hard plastic mask which, although not comfortable, did wonders for my skin.

Everything I learnt to do at the clinic helped me become more comfortable *in* my skin and *with* my skin and I took the big step of going without my mask in public. And you know what – no one even looked twice. I also regained some of my old Turia confidence – I can speak a bit of French (albeit badly) so it was me that ordered our meals, gave instructions to the taxi drivers and organised our weekends etc.

Coming home we arrived in Sydney at 11 pm at night and had to leave first thing in the morning as I had been booked to speak at the Shoalhaven Women's Conference. There were about 300 women and I received my first ever standing ovation. I spoke about my experiences before the fire and leading up to it and what I remembered about the day. Then I gave an overview of my time in hospital and subsequent rehabilitation. Here is how I ended my speech:

> I'm not saying that this experience has been a walk in the park. I'm not saying that I never lost it, that I never lashed out at the people I loved, or that I didn't break down in tears when confronted with the reality of my journey. But overall, I tried to remain positive and optimistic about the future.
>
> And what is there not to be optimistic about? After all, there is a lot of hope for burn survivors these days – if doctors can change Michael Jackson's skin colour, surely there's a lot of things they can do to improve our quality of life. My brainy surgeons can do anything – even turn a man into a woman, and a woman into a man. I think making me a new nose will be relatively easy by comparison. Although, as my surgeon has told me, I will look like a werewolf for a period of three weeks following my nose operation. When I asked if I would be able to go outside, he advised only if I wanted to scare the little kiddies away.

I put up with all the operations because I focus on having a better result. Sometimes you need to take one step back to move two steps forward. As technology improves at its current exponential rate, my clever surgeons will be able to do more and more. I'll probably have surgeries for the rest of my life. But that's simply because I never give up – I want the best results, and I'll do anything to get them. I've actually just returned from a six-week stint at a burns clinic in France, and I reckon my family will be blown away by the improvements in my skin when they see them.

So, where am I now? I reckon we live in one of the most beautiful places in Australia, I've got great support from my family and friends, and I've got the best partner in the world. I'm studying my Masters in Engineering, I'm working towards an MBA and I'm also writing a book. I've got plenty of goals for the future, such as having a family with Michael. For now though, I'm focusing on my upcoming operations as well as the 20km Lake Argyle swim, which will take part in this time next year.

When I think about what happened to me, a lot of questions spring to mind. Was it fate that I was there in the fire? Maybe I have a different purpose in life now. Or maybe I was simply in the wrong place at the wrong time. I don't have the answers to any of those questions, and I don't think anyone really knows until they cross over. But I do believe in making the best out of your circumstances. Never ever give up. Life can deal you some rotten cards sometimes, but it's how you play which is important.

I was so excited that everyone had enjoyed my speech; it gave me confidence for a future in public speaking.

I have come a long way from the total despair days in the Concord Burns Unit. Naturally anyone reading my story will know what amazing love and support I have had from my family – I don't know many mums who are as cool as mine. I have had Dad and Genji to help me get strong and younger brothers to make me laugh; they were both shorter than me when I went to Kununurrra, but now tower over me. They are still so sweet and kind – nothing is too much trouble. But to have the love of someone like Michael is beyond special. And he must owe much of his lovely nature to his parents, Julie and Gary.

I've gone from not being able to do anything much when I first came home to having a really busy life. I particularly like studying, so I've been keeping my brain active. In 2012 I started my Masters degree in Mining Engineering at the University of New South Wales, and in 2013 I enrolled to do my Masters of Business Administration with Southern Cross University. My days are extremely full – physio, the LPG machine, facial exercises, yoga, personal training, study and socialising.

When I came home I was afraid that everyone would treat me differently, even friends. But to my relief that didn't happen. My close friends have all been fantastic and I wouldn't have come as far without them. One of the things that I like about my friends is their sense of humour. When I told Briggs that I was worried about my left wedding ring finger being amputated she said, 'Well, at least you'll still be able to give people the bird (make the rude stick finger)!'

But I have to say that former peripheral friends have dropped off the radar (which is fine) and I did find the attitudes of some people rather unenlightened – for instance I was pretty annoyed when people told me they thought I was sitting at home bored all day. Anyone who *really* knows me, knows I can never be bored, I always have a million things to do. Then there were other blinkered individuals who pretended that nothing had happened to me and just talked about the parties that they had been to.

I have been blown away by the support the Ulladulla community has shown for me. This is probably best demonstrated by the Masquerade Ball in Ulladulla that my mates (and in particular Briggs and Nicola) organised in April 2012 to raise funds for my medical and other expenses. They decided to make it a masquerade ball in deference to me having to wear a mask. It was a sell-out for 500 people, and that's huge for Ulladulla. Michael drove me to the Community Centre, where the ball was in full swing, and I was overwhelmed. I gave a little speech but I was still very frail and tired easily and we left after an hour. I was so grateful for everyone's efforts; it was this event that gave us the funds to pay for the trip to France.

One of the more unexpected positives to come out of such a terrible event is the friendship that has developed between me and the others who met for the first time that day. Over the last year Kate and I have become quite close and email each other regularly. I saw Hully and Hal in Sydney shortly after I came out of hospital and we (Michael and me) struck up a rapport with both of them and have continued to stay in touch. In November 2012, Hully, Hal, Kate and her friend Andrew, who had been a volunteer on the day of the fire, and Michael and I rented a house in Ulladulla for a weekend. We hung out together for the first time since the fire and it was fantastic. We were in good spirits and we drank a few beers, ate pizza, played board games and just relaxed. We did speak about the fire and compared scars but we didn't focus on it. I was so proud of Kate – she seemed to be one hundred per cent independent and I was bit jealous of that, but I was also proud of how far I'd come in my own independence since we saw each other at the inquiry. I think she was proud of me too.

I had just got my licence back – it had expired while I was in hospital – and I played tour guide and drove them around my beautiful Ulladulla. Michael went fishing on the Sunday and the rest of us just cruised the beaches and I showed them the great surfing places, we had coffee at a local winery and later we visited Michael's parents. I know they liked meeting everyone they'd heard so much about. We plan to do the 20-kilometre Lake Argyle swim together.

Driving again was cool. It was funny seeing the looks on people's faces as I drove around Ulladulla wearing my black face mask in our blue Holden commodore station wagon (Michael sold the little blue Hyundai). In the early months, when I appeared in public and people stared I would be a bit upset – Michael would say they were only looking because I had the best boyfriend. I didn't mind if it was children looking, that's natural curiosity, but when adults came up to me in the street and asked what happened I was a bit pissed off, thinking they just wanted to sticky beak. I'm less sensitive now and realise people just wanted to know; their interest wasn't malicious.

In a way wearing the mask has been a positive – it has raised the profile of burns injuries and that flows on to the issue of skin and tissue donation. When I'm out in public and people look at me, I know many will recognise me from the publicity: 'See that girl in the mask – she's the girl who was caught in that fire.' Kate was just as badly burnt as me but because she wasn't burnt on her face, people don't immediately associate her with the fire in the Kimberley.

At the beginning of 2013, I felt I was getting to a good stage of my journey. I stopped crying and started laughing again; I'm a bit like Mum and love to laugh, and every time I laughed I could see Michael's face light up, hearing the old Turia. I didn't need to medicate my pain any more.

Some things I will never be able to do and some things I can never get back; for instance, due to my damaged skin I can't regulate my body temperature (one of the main functions of skin) so when it's cold I'm really cold and when it's hot, I'm hot. This will never get better but that's okay because it doesn't affect the major areas that matter. While I was in hospital, sometimes I would ask Michael to put blankets on me and once he covered me with a total of eight blankets! Then at night I would be burning up and sweating and kick off all my blankets. I would occasionally get so hot that I would ask the nurses to put ice packs on my groin and under my arm pits.

My future with Michael will be different to the one I envisaged. Although the skin on my stomach was shaved to provide grafts to burnt areas, I can still have children. However I will probably need help with a baby – maybe a nanny for warming bottles and other tricky movements. Michael and I bought an apartment in Mollymook near Ulladulla in March 2013 and I did all the negotiating. Since coming back from France we have had a great time decorating it.

When I think about what has happened to me I link it to my long-felt desire to 'make a difference'. Briggs reminded me that when we were teenagers I said I wanted to make a name for myself doing something worthwhile one day; someone who did something that was meaningful to society; in no way did I think this life-changing trauma would be the way I would be known publicly.

Of course I have asked the question 'Why me?' – wouldn't anyone in my position? But the other side of me has always answered, 'Why not me?' I knew I was a good person before this happened to me so I asked myself why I was being tested. What was this agony for? I survived the school bus crash when I was a teenager and I survived the fire; there has to be some meaning in my ability to survive. How could I make something meaningful out of this and validate what happened? I realised that one way would be to help others who need donated skin like I did. I was dumbfounded when I found out that there was no skin available in Australia to help me and that the skin that saved my life had to come from an unknown donor on the other side of the world. I want to raise awareness for skin and tissue donation in Australia in the hope that skin banks will always have enough supplies to help save other lives.

I hope that telling my story goes some way to helping this aim and to inspire others who have challenging issues in their lives. I'm confident about becoming a motivational speaker; I have become an unofficial ambassador for DonateLife and have started to advocate the need for organ and tissue donation.

Since I contacted DonateLife I have been involved with a couple of its events; I was invited to the launch of the 2013 DonateLife Week at Kirribilli House in Sydney and again to Canberra later to take part in the DonateLife Walk. In June 2014, I plan to trek the Inca Trail in Peru to raise money for Interplast – a not-for-profit organisation in which Professor Haertsch is a volunteer medical specialist. Interplast provides medical treatment for people in the Asia-Pacific region who are disabled as a result of congenital or acquired medical conditions, such as cleft lip and palate or burn scar contractures. Some of my friends, including Briggs, Nicola, Michael's sister Shae, my friend Mary Kavanagh from Kununurra and another friend, Shae Clayton, are planning to join me.

I've accepted the way I look now, although it's not perfect – yet. One day I will look beautiful again; that is, beautiful to me, because the people I love say I am beautiful to them anyway. Surgery will be ongoing and I will probably have surgical corrections for the rest of my life. In the beginning my surgery was based around function. But in the future it will be based around appearance. There will probably be little things I'm not happy with because I'm a perfectionist. As medical technology for burns improves, there will no doubt be many more things the doctors can do for me. I know it will be a couple of years before I can surf again and a couple of years before I'm confident enough to wear shorts. All of that aesthetic stuff will take time but I'm still young and I have a long life ahead of me and I have more ambitious plans for the future; I want to gain my doctorate in Engineering and go back to work in mining. I also want to become an endurance athlete: I want to run another ultramarathon; I want to compete in an ironman. I am dedicated to raising awareness for skin donation and I would like to see a burns rehabilitation centre, similar to the one in France, set up in Australia. I have so much to do . . . you might say I have gone from the despair of not wanting to live to having everything to live for.

SEVENTEEN

THE RIPPLE EFFECT

THIRTEEN PEOPLE DIRECTLY FACED THE FIRE IN THE KIMBERLEY on 2 September 2011; but it irrevocably changed the lives of many more. The ripples cast a wide circle. At the core were Turia and Kate, the two young women who nearly lost their lives.

Turia, the most profoundly injured, tells her story in this book. Her survival is nothing short of a miracle and her brave determination to live a life that is as normal as possible is inspirational.

Kate spent nearly six months in Melbourne's Alfred Hospital recovering from extensive burns to most of her body. Like Turia, Kate became infected and because she had very little unburnt skin from which to harvest skin for grafting, the grafting took many months. She has undergone more than thirty operations on her hands, which are clawed due to contracture, and she lost her right index finger. Her doctors wanted to amputate her left leg below the knee but she fought to keep it, though she did lose half her left foot. She also lost most of her ear lobes.

She has not been able to return to work. When she left hospital she had to wear a special vacuum pack weighing

4 kilograms on her foot for eight months. She was finally fitted for a prosthetic foot in January 2013. Her injuries meant her driver's licence was cancelled; until she got it back she was isolated and had to rely on others to drive her around as she does not live near public transport. Kate was previously very fit and loved adventure events. Today she can't even ride a bike because she can't grip the handlebars and can't reach the pedals. In 2013 Kate had to make an unenviable choice: to have her hand amputated or to have her fingers fused together permanently. She chose the latter.

Because of her high media profile following the fire and a misunderstanding, Kate also distressingly become known as 'the girl with two boyfriends'. When she decided to enter the race, ten months in advance of the event, she was not in a relationship and on the entry form listed her ex-partner and her mother as next of kin to contact in case of an emergency. At the time of the race she was in a new relationship but forgot to change the next-of-kin details. At Kununurra Hospital she knew she was going into an induced coma and wanted to put her new boyfriend's name as contact but couldn't remember his mobile number – understandable in the circumstances.

Dr Brandee Waite contacted the people named on Kate's form. The ex-partner went to the hospital with Kate's mother to anxiously await Kate's arrival from Darwin. Two days later, Kate's new partner read about what happened to her in the newspaper and immediately went to the hospital. (Kate had been going to stay on in Western Australia after the race and do some sightseeing with her friends Andrew Baker and Hal, so he wasn't worried that he hadn't heard from her.) When he arrived at the hospital it was a little confronting for the two men. Kate was in a coma and not able to explain the mix-up.

But a hospital is a hotbed of gossip and word that she had two boyfriends went viral; more than eighteen months later she was still being stopped by people asking: 'Aren't you the girl with the two boyfriends?' Her new partner was very supportive and did whatever he could when Kate left hospital but after a couple of months, Kate felt she could no longer sustain the relationship. She wanted to get on with the business of adjusting to her much altered life.

Michael Hull – now affectionately called 'Hully' by the rest of the group – was flown to Royal Perth Hospital. He had a combination of first-, second- and third-degree burns: he suffered burns on both legs from ankle to knee, plus his fingers and ears as well as his arms to the elbow. He underwent skin grafts and wore pressure garments on his arms and legs for many months. He has a long permanent scar on his right leg, where he cut himself while running through the fire.

Hully had ongoing pain and continued to receive rehabilitation in Sydney for nine months after the Kimberley disaster. To focus on something other than his injuries, he began to train for other adventurous events. In April 2012 he did a seven-day trek to the North Pole, dragging a heavy sled; in September the same year he competed in a marathon in the Flinders Ranges in Victoria with Hal. In 2013 he competed in an Iron Man triathlon in New Zealand; the Marathon des Sables, a 250-kilometre ultramarathon in Morocco; and walked the Kokoda Trail with friends.

Martin Van der Merwe suffered thirty-five per cent burns on both calves to mid-thigh and substantial burns to his right hand. He returned to Ghana after three weeks in Royal Perth Hospital. He has recovered well and is running again and playing squash, cycling and swimming. But not a day goes by when he doesn't think about Turia and Kate and how such young lives could be so tragically affected.

Hal was diagnosed with post-traumatic stress disorder and symptoms of reactive depression. Like Hully, he came to the conclusion that the best way forward was to compete again. Two months after the ill-fated Kimberley run he competed in the nine-day Adventure Racing World Championships in Tasmania. In 2012 he did a marathon in the Flinders Ranges with Hully and has competed in two forty-eight-hour adventure races, two ultramarathons of 100 kilometres and another nine-day race in the Flinders Ranges.

Shaun too was profoundly affected by the events of that day in which he thought his father had died. He believes he is a better person now but would not have chosen what happened as a way of learning one of life's lessons. He values his time with his family more than ever, conscious that he could never know when it might be the last time. After his experience with RtP, Shaun is less trusting of adventure event organisers: he is selective about the events he enters, thoroughly checking out the background of the organiser first. He is disappointed that the event company is still able to operate – apparently not held to account for any of the shortcomings identified by the inquiry in its report.

The negative effects didn't stop with those who lived through the fire on the ridge; many others were caught up in this tragic, preventable event. The founder of the company, Mary Gadams, herself received second-degree burns to her fingers and the backs of her arms and legs. After being initially treated in Kununurra Hospital she flew back to her home in Hong Kong.

Then there were those who escaped the fire, three of whom saw Turia and Kate engulfed by flames, and some who went to extraordinary efforts to get help. Many competitors were also caught up in the drama and aftermath.

Some of those people have been so traumatised that even today they find it difficult to talk about what happened. The three Newcrest miners, all tough men, went to ground after the initial publicity, deeply affected by what they had seen – and the images they continue to live with. They were hailed as heroes by those they helped after the fire; but that's not the way they saw themselves. They have all moved out of the region and don't speak to the media.

Volunteer Lon Croot lives with the image of the fire overcoming competitors and the sounds of the screams. He also lives with the frustrating knowledge that his concerns about the fires burning out course markers on certain parts of the route in the days before the race were not taken seriously by RtP organisers, even though he was a local; at the subsequent inquiry, when asked if there had been adequate risk identification, Lon recounted events from a few days before the race: 'They said to me that some of the ribbons had been burnt off and they had to go back and re-tie the ribbons along the track. I said . . . "Are you worried about that?" . . . If the wind picks up, I was a little concerned . . . but I was at the bottom of the ladder. I do not think the fires were taken into account enough as a danger.' One of the questions he was asked during the hearing was if there was any briefing about what to do if there was a fire. He told the committee: 'There was definitely no briefing . . .'[1]

Ellis Caffin and Heather Scott, who so narrowly escaped the fire, did everything in their power to raise the alarm only to be trapped in an ongoing nightmare. When they finally reached checkpoint two and found it was burnt out, they set off for checkpoint three; they tried to hail a lift and discovered outback hospitality selective.

Cars in the outback are few and far between. A couple stopped and, although Ellis begged for help, explaining the situation, he and Heather were refused a lift; the drivers were not going their way. Ellis and Heather may have looked hot and dishevelled: they were desperate to get help; they had run out of water during their 6-kilometre trek back to checkpoint two and were grateful they managed to find some in a creek. Another man, in a ute, told them he was a landowner and said the fire was a controlled burn deliberately lit to prevent bigger fires during the dry season.

At last two campers in a third vehicle cheerily told them to hop in. As they were driving they came across a large group of people waiting by the side of the road. Ellis and Heather discovered that most were competitors who had been behind them and had all heeded Ellis's call from the valley to turn around. RacingthePlanet staff had tried to evacuate everyone from checkpoint two at 2 pm but did not have enough transport; eventually everyone was moved to the main road with the help of a passing local resident in a troop carrier; they were left with some water and one race official and told to wait while staff headed off inland towards where they thought the competitors may have been trapped. Someone would pick them up later. It was by then 7 pm.

No one had any means of communication; they did not know if the girls on the ridge had been rescued and had no idea when or if anyone was coming back for them. Among the group were Brenda and Martyn Sawyer and Lon Croot, who had alerted RtP at checkpoint two about the fire and the likelihood of burns victims. Lon was still suffering from shock after witnessing what he believed was someone engulfed in flames but he was frustrated by the delay; he had been keen to go back and see what he could do to help but had been told to stay put by RtP staff and, not being in charge, felt obliged to do so.

For Heather and Ellis, their seven-hour ordeal was not over. They were suffering from smoke inhalation and left the group deciding to press on and walk on to the nearby Great Northern Highway, where they managed to hitch another lift to the nearest town of Wyndham, about a thirty-minute drive away. After Ellis and Heather were treated at Wyndham Hospital, they made their own way back to Kununurra, where they discovered that Turia and Kate had been rescued but their injuries were life-threatening.

Heather has remained deeply traumatised by the events of that day. And for many months afterwards, she cried every time she talked about it. In the statement she made to the police on 6 September 2011, she described how the day after the race she and Ellis returned to the course to retrieve an expensive camera they had dropped, and were guided by a Kununurra local who had been attached to the media team. He mentioned that the media team had been aware of the bush fire about two to three hours before it had come through the area and had made a decision only to film for one hour before moving to safety. The question has gone through her mind so often: why were the runners allowed to go through checkpoint two when so many people already knew that there was danger.[2]

Rod Rutherford, who loves extreme adventure events and has competed in ultramarathons in other parts of the world, now has a fear of fire he never had before. He rarely talks about his terrifying encounter with the fast-approaching flames as he finds it difficult to express the raw emotion. He gets distressed when he recalls trickling water into Turia's mouth while he was on the ridge with the others and cried when the first *60 Minutes* program brought back the memories of it all. He recalls vividly holding back the door of the helicopter while the others struggled to get Turia on board. Rod thinks about Turia and Kate every day.

Helicopter pilot Paul Cripps, who carried out the risky rescue of Turia and Kate, speaks movingly of the experience: 'Thinking back to the day of the tragedy, it was not until Bryn and I were on our way out to Tier Range that the adrenaline started to pump through my body. I knew from the conversations I had that afternoon with Nathan Summers that it was going to be difficult but it's not until you are on your way to the scene that you really start to think about just how you are going to tackle such a challenging task. I had done several medivacs in some fairly confined spaces – but not from the side of a cliff with no space to land a helicopter.

'The high risk of the operation kept going through my mind and I did not want to put more lives at risk, including my own and Bryn's; I thought of my wife and son back in Kununurra several times that afternoon. I didn't want to leave my wife to raise our son on her own because I made a stupid mistake or took an unnecessary risk.

'Apart from the limited performance of the aircraft in the hot conditions in the Kimberley, I also had to consider how many people we needed on board the helicopter conducting a high-risk operation which is why I decided to lift Turia and Kate off the site separately; if something were to go wrong, at least the number of lives lost would be reduced.

'I often think of that day with a mix of emotions. I feel for Kate and Turia and their long battle to recover. I feel angry that they spent so long out in extreme temperatures, which is essentially due to poor communication. And I think of myself sitting there in my air-conditioned comfortable office while they sat on that cliff with the sun beating down on them, flies and ants crawling over their horrific burns, waiting for someone to come and help them, waiting for someone to take the pain away, or at the very least ease the pain.

'People say it's easy to look back and say "what if", but is it really that easy to look back and realise that perhaps two beautiful girls wouldn't be facing a lifetime of recovery if the risk of fire had been considered! I don't think that's an easy thing to think about at all.'

Turia's family and friends have been affected for life.

Turia's mother, Célestine, a spiritual woman with an ingrained positivity, kept it together in front of her precious daughter for a year and a half. In the beginning she dreamt of the 'old Turia'; Turia would always come into the dream and tell her, 'Mum, she's gone.' The only time Turia saw Célestine cry was the day of that first walk in the Burns Unit corridor, when the sight of Turia shuffling along painfully was just too much to bear.

Célestine kept her tears for the night, sobbing into her pillow. John, her comforting rock, would sometimes slip into another room to get some sleep so he could get up for work at 5.30 am. Célestine staved off her major emotional meltdown till the day Turia and Michael flew to France for Turia's specialist treatment in March 2013. She was immobilised for two weeks: she couldn't cook, eat, talk or sleep – only stand in the shower for hours and sob.

Genji, the strong, gung-ho military man, still cries over what happened to his beloved little sister. Turia's younger brothers, Heimanu and Toriki, were heartbroken about their 'Sissy'. Happy teenage years went on hold. Turia's survival and recovery became everyone's focus and the boys had to mature very quickly. In 2012, Heimanu turned sixteen; he didn't like to ask if he could have a birthday party in the middle of such sadness but he asked anyway. Célestine was too distracted to think about parties. Finally she thought, 'He must have his party.' And Célestine gave him one – for eighty guests – friends and family.

Michael took his daughter to the Xtreme Fitness gym in Ulladulla wearing her black face mask and worked with her to help her regain muscle strength. He saw tears in the eyes of grown men working out as they saw her determination and her pain and effort. He too cried but not in front of Turia; he had to remain strong and supportive – the dad who had always encouraged her to do more, to try harder. While having his golden girl damaged to this degree was enormously sad, infuriating and frustrating, he was nevertheless uplifted by her tenacity and her willingness to forge ahead with her irrevocably altered life.

And the love of Turia's life, Michael Hoskin, thinks about what happened every day; he has been totally shattered about what happened to his girl. He has learnt to stay sane and deal with his emotions by running and swimming. He does not cry in front of Turia. Sometimes he goes alone to the beach and sits on the sand looking out at the waves and tears roll down his face. After several minutes he will push the memory away and refocus on their future.

Every time Turia has surgery, he wishes he could lie on the operating table for her; his stomach churns until he gets the call to say it's over and the surgery went well. There is a part of Michael that has been scarred forever from witnessing first-hand the trauma Turia has endured.

Michael's parents too, the calm and easygoing Gary

and Julie, felt an overwhelming sadness during the year Turia lived with them. Turia never saw Julie cry but others did. Janine Austen did when Julie asked her to be Turia's physiotherapist. Every day for months, when Julie struggled to keep her feelings around Turia in check, she would walk with two friends late in the day. And she'd walk, talk and cry. Turia didn't see Gary cry either, but cry he did. Gary and Julie watched with admiration Turia's determined struggle to become independent and took pride in their son's patient and devoted care of her. At the same time they had to deal with insensitive comments from a few local people who asked why Michael, such a good-looking young guy, had stuck by Turia.

Turia's best friends, Briggs and Nicola, live with the image of their friend, her head the size of a football, lying unconscious in the Concord Intensive Care Unit early in the morning after she arrived from Darwin. These two positive, happy young women, still devastated by that image, now focus on their belief that the Turia they know will 'get on top of it' because 'that's Turia'.

So many people affected. So many questions about how it came to be that an international event company could have put the lives of its competitors, volunteers and staff in danger.

EIGHTEEN

HOLDING
RESPONSIBILITY

LIKE TURIA'S FAMILY, KATE SANDERSON'S FAMILY WANTED answers. Kate's older brother, Ian Sanderson, an IT specialist at a Perth university, took up the baton to hunt for the truth and make sure such a preventable tragedy was never repeated. The more questions he asked and the more he discovered, the more determined he became to push for a formal government inquiry, especially as the event had State Government sponsorship. Western Australia is one of only two States in Australia in which the coroner does not have the power to investigate a fire unless there is a death. Fortunately Ian's sister, Kate, and Turia did not die but he felt someone should be held responsible for what he saw as deeply flawed event organisation.

In the months immediately following the catastrophe, he regularly appeared in the media calling for accountability and became a constant thorn in the side of the Western Australian Government. Ian, a former military man, said on one TV appearance that had he still been in the army, and had he organised an event with an outcome such as the September 2011 Kimberley Ultramarathon, he would have been court-martialled.

He flew to Hong Kong in January 2012, met Mary Gadams of RacingthePlanet at the airport and put to her a series of questions relating to the event, most of which she declined to answer.

In the weeks after the race, Western Australia's Fire and Emergency Services Authority (FESA) and the Western Australia Police Arson Squad conducted a joint investigation into the fire, during which more than forty witness statements were taken. Given Turia's and Kate's life-threatening injuries, it was thought prudent to collect this information in case of a coronial inquest if either woman died.

The cause of the fire wasn't established but it was found to have started about five days beforehand, around 12 kilometres southeast from where the competitors were burnt. It had 'meandered'[1] slowly until it reached the Tier Gorge, where its intensity increased significantly, assisted by a wind change plus a very high fuel load: because it was also the hot season in the far north, the grass was tinder dry and easily combustible. Its spread accelerated as it climbed the walls of the gorge, which provided a tunnelling effect for the prevailing easterly winds.[2]

As communications, or lack thereof, was emerging as a serious issue, Ian probed further. He found RtP used a mixture of Iridium, Thuraya and other systems for satellite phones. This was confirmed by Mary Gadams when Ian met her in Hong Kong – one of the few questions she did answer as she was confident that RtP had covered its communications well. She was probably unaware of how knowledgable Ian was in this area – in his previous career he had been heavily involved in IT and communications support for the NATO mission in Afghanistan. In this role he had evaluated Iridium, Thuraya and the Inmarsat BGAN systems.

Next Ian did some fact-finding with Telstra and was told they recommend Iridium as the only reliable sat phone for use in outback regions in Australia such as the Kimberley. Where Thuraya uses geostationary satellites, which cause significant time delays in voice calls in an outback situation, Iridium uses low earth-orbit satellites, which have time delays closer to that of ordinary cellular phone calls. Thuraya is also more expensive to use in Australia, as Telstra has discounted air time with Iridium. After gathering this information, Ian doubted that RtP had fully understood the technology.

Telstra maintains a pool of Iridium handsets for loan, which would have been available to RtP if they had requested them. Ian found that if Telstra had been asked, its advice would have been to only use Iridium. He knew that RtP had brought some Iridium handsets with them, although not enough to equip every checkpoint and every mobile member of staff.[3] Introducing Thuraya handsets into the mix had added significant complexity and risk to communications because of the difficulties of getting Thuraya and Iridium to work together. However it could have been useful if every checkpoint and vehicle had carried both types of sat phone and had an agreed protocol for the use of each.

Ian also came across some discontent from local volunteers over the way the event was organised in the week prior to the race. One volunteer told him in an emotional email that RtP constantly put him 'on the spot' because of its 'cost-cutting', which was 'a big issue for us locals as it gave us hurdles to cross on a daily basis'. The volunteer said he personally had a top-of-the-range Iridium sat phone but RtP didn't want to hire Iridium sat phones because they were given some 'useless Thuraya phones' by the

Western Australian Government as part of its sponsorship arrangement. He says RtP officials told him on a number of occasions throughout the race preparation week that the Kimberley was one of the only places in the world where RtP didn't have phone reception.

Initially Ian encountered a great deal of government resistance to a formal inquiry. He had meetings and corresponded with members of parliament, in particular the Deputy Premier, Dr Kim Hames, who held the twin portfolios of Tourism and Health, and the Premier, Colin Barnett. Many reasons were offered – and documented in letters to Ian – as to why the government didn't have the jurisdiction to conduct an inquiry. Dr Hames also suggested that the push for an inquiry was really about compensation for the victims;[4] compensation was not something Ian had raised with anyone. The possibility that the government's tourism arm, Tourism WA, could be found to hold some responsibility for the event's dreadful outcome was never articulated.

Ian's dogged persistence found a sympathetic ear with the Labor Opposition, in particular the Member of the Legislative Assembly who held the Opposition's tourism portfolio, Michelle Roberts. Mrs Roberts, with the backing of the Opposition, came up with a plan to ambush the House on the opening day of the new session of parliament – the last before the forthcoming State election. Premier Barnett gave his opening speech, after which it fell to the Opposition to respond. Labor had just elected a new leader, Mark MacGowan, so there was a great deal of media interest in how he would perform at the opening session.

To the Government's surprise, Mark MacGowan ceded the floor to Michelle Roberts. She got up to speak and opened with the words, 'A grave injustice has been done to a group of people who participated in an event in this State last September. I am of course referring to the Kimberley Ultramarathon. The injustice is that the Western Australian Government has failed to call an independent inquiry into the event . . .'[5] She continued her speech, outlining in detail the injuries to the young athletes, how the events unfolded during the day and the rescue; she also read a statement from Kate about what happened to her. The usual background House chatter gradually stopped until you could have heard a pin drop.

'The race had a number of points spread over a long distance. What specific medical or safety preparations were made by organisers, including local medical and retrieval services, in the preparation phase and how effective was communication between race staff, competitors and those services during the race itself? Only by holding an inquiry will the Government move beyond the weasel words of false compassion. Only by holding an inquiry will the Government reassure visitors to this State that if they come and compete in an event and are seriously injured, through no fault of their own, that they will have some measure of justice . . .'[6]

The thirty-one-minute address to the House concluded: 'Only by holding an inquiry will the Government begin to act with proper authentic compassion to two young women whose lives have been so terribly changed and to their families and friends.'[7]

Debate followed, during which the Government's argument against an inquiry became weaker until it finally collapsed; the Opposition was acknowledged to have made its case.

Ian Sanderson, sitting in the gallery, had watched with interest, noting that Kim Hames, looking uncomfortable, left the chamber during a large part of Mrs Roberts' speech.

Afterwards, when she turned, looked up and gave Ian the victory thumbs-up, it was all he could do to choke back the tears. It was the day Kate left hospital after nearly six months and one of the most emotional days of his life.

Two weeks later, the five Legislative Assembly members that made up the Government's Economics and Industry Standing Committee were tasked with investigating RacingthePlanet's 2011 Kimberley Ultramarathon. The committee was given three months to report to the House of Representatives. Michelle Roberts was co-opted to sit on the committee, bringing its number to six.

The 2011 ultramarathon of 2 September was the second event the Hong Kong-based RtP had organised in the far north of Western Australia. In April of the previous year it had held a 250-kilometre seven-day event in the same Kimberley region. In the ten years prior to the 2011 event, RtP had staged more than thirty-three foot races in eight countries.[8]

For the 2011 race, RtP had secured a sponsorship arrangement with Eventscorp, the Western Australian Government's events agency and a division of Tourism WA. The sponsorship money came from an allocation of funds from the tourism body to foster adventure sports in Western Australia. The sponsorship agreement with RtP, which gained final government approval on 22 August 2011, was for an amount of up to $105,000 for one year with an option for a further two years provided certain contract milestones were met (one of which was a minimum number of competitors). RacingthePlanet signed off on the sponsorship agreement on 1 September, the day before the race.[9]

A contract worth a further $170,000 was signed with documentary film makers Beyond Action to record the ultramarathon as part of Tourism WA's media coverage of the event.[10] The footage was to be used to promote the region through the development and distribution of television programs and documentaries both in Australia and internationally.

The committee was asked to examine the actions of the organiser, RtP, and to consider if RtP took all reasonable steps to identify and reduce risks and maintain the safety of competitors, employees, contractors, spectators and volunteers in the preparation for and running of the event. This included its response to the fire and the injuries, access to medical support and evacuations. Its terms of reference also included an examination of the roles and actions of a range of government bodies before, during and after the event. Among these bodies was Tourism WA, the Department of Environment and Conservation (DEC), the Department of Health (DOH), the Kununurra Shire Fire and Emergency Services Authority (FESA), Western Australia Police, the Department of Regional Development and Lands (DRDL), St John's Ambulance and the Kununurra Visitors Centre (KVC).

Other individuals were invited to appear, including representatives from other ultra-events organisations, local landholders, the Heliwork WA pilots, race volunteers and competitors. The committee received thirty-three submissions; forty-one people appeared before the committee during the hearings in April and May. The injured competitors were invited to appear on April 30.

Turia was determined to attend and give her evidence in person. It was a huge effort for her to fly to Perth; she had only been out of hospital for three months and was extremely fragile. Sitting in her pressure suit for the five-hour flight was agony and even going to the toilet posed problems. She and Michael flew to Perth the day before she was to appear and were joined by Kate, who had flown across from Melbourne and was greeted by Ian. Hully arrived back from his trek to the North Pole just in time to fly over for the hearing and Shaun, who lived in Perth, was there: he had elected to give evidence on behalf of his father in Africa. Hal offered to come from Sydney too but was advised he wouldn't be needed.

When the session for the competitors' evidence formally opened, the media were permitted in to take photos but then all cameramen were asked to leave. Journalists were allowed but there could be no recording devices. Apart from the competitors, media, committee and their researchers, the only other people present were Michael Hoskin, and Greg Walsh, the Sydney lawyer representing Turia Pitt, Michael Hull, Hal Benson and Martin Van der Merwe, and Peter Burke, the Melbourne lawyer representing Kate Sanderson. The session was streamed live on the internet.

By then the committee had already heard a great deal of evidence; they had spent time in Kununurrra talking to locals; and had even flown over the region and viewed the site of the fire and where the competitors had been trapped so had formed a good understanding of what had happened on the day. But nothing could have prepared them for the sight of Turia and Kate. When the two women walked into the room together holding hands, the expressions on the faces of everyone told their own story. Suddenly it was real. No one had seen them before: Turia, stick thin, her face covered by a black mask with only her eyes, mouth and nose tip showing and hands with missing fingers. And Kate, limping in a big black boot, hands clawed and scarred. This was the photo that went out to the world; an image that shocked.

When Turia walked in, the impact on Shaun was overwhelming. He said hello to her but she was too fragile for a hug and he hurriedly left the room for a few minutes to gather his emotions; he couldn't hold back the tears. Shaun was not a man to wear his heart on his sleeve but seeing Turia brought back that terrible day and everything came to the surface. Hully told him later it was a good thing and part of the healing process. But Shaun could only think that nothing could properly heal Turia's injuries.

Mary Gadams appeared two days later. Part of her evidence was given in a closed session and not streamed live. Ian Sanderson attended the hearing but his presence was carefully managed so the two did not have an opportunity to meet face to face.

Invited to make a brief opening statement, the RtP CEO began reading out a carefully crafted statement – around twelve pages long. Committee members commented several times on how time-consuming this was, reminding Gadams that the purpose of the hearing was for them to put questions to her, and that there had been ample opportunity to submit written statements prior to the hearing.[11] They also had to remind her legal representative not to try to answer questions on Gadams' behalf.[12]

Turia, Michael, Kate, Hully and Shaun had not been aware that the RtP owner was flying to Australia to appear that day. As their own evidence was streamed live, they believed she must have known they were also in Perth. They were extremely disappointed she did not make personal contact with them then or since.

Michael was also upset when he later read Gadams' response to the committee's question: 'What responsibility, if any, did RacingthePlanet take for the injuries to Turia and Kate and the others and if it intended to do anything to assist them in the future?',[13] Gadams replied that Racingthe Planet did not know who was liable for the injuries. She said that while their medical director, Dr Waite, had been in touch with the families there had 'never been a time when I have had an email or call or anything from any member in the family where I said that I would not meet. I remain open to meet with any of the families'.[14]

The committee then put to Gadams: 'So that is all you intend to do in the future to assist them?' Gadams replied: 'I mean, no one has come to us to ask us for anything, and if someone comes to ask us, you know, I am willing to meet at any time.'[15]

After obtaining an extension, the committee sat for five months and handed down its report on 16 August 2012. It was the last possible date that would ensure a government response before the parliament rose for the summer recess; after that each committee member would return to the preoccupation of the next State election.

Just prior to the release of the committee's findings, Mary Gadams made a pre-emptive strike by issuing a statement to *The Australian* denying any liability and hitting out at Western Australian Government agencies for their 'lack of co-ordination and disregard for fire risk'.[16] Gadams said the only way the tragedy could have been averted was 'to not hold the event in Western Australia in the first place'.[17]

'The truth is, we simply would not have had a race there if we thought there was any risk of fire injuring human beings,' she told *The Australian*. 'One of the issues in the Kimberley or Western Australia is who is doing what or who you should contact. In most countries the police is the central agency. How are the tourists in the Kimberley to know there's fire risk? There was no warning anywhere.'[18]

That was an interesting statement from Mary Gadams considering the many warnings – and advice about whom to contact – issued in the lead-up to the event.[19] As for 'not knowing there's a fire risk', that too was a puzzling statement when RtP team members had been coming across fires in the days before the event and local volunteers expressed concerns about the potential dangers of those fires.[20]

The committee examined all aspects of the 2011 Kimberley Ultramarathon and made thirty-five findings; notably it found that RtP did not take all reasonable steps to identify risks, reduce risks or maintain the safety of competitors, employees, contractors, spectators and volunteers in the 2011 Kimberley Ultramarathon.[21]

One of the key findings was that because RtP was aware there had been fires on and in the vicinity of the course prior to and on the day of the race, it should have been aware of the risks that posed. The international standard for risk management (ISO 31000:2009) was a reasonable benchmark but RtP's management and risk assessment plan and its risk identification process for the Kimberley Ultramarathon were not consistent with that standard.[22] This finding was based on several factors:

- RacingthePlanet did not involve people with appropriate knowledge in identifying risks associated with the event nor communicate and consult adequately with relevant agencies and individuals on its management and risk assessment plan.
- The risks identified in RtP's management and risk assessment plan appeared to be generic and were notably lacking in causes and consequences.
- RacingthePlanet did not contact FESA about fires it had

seen in the days leading up to the race, despite being asked to do so by the KVC and the DEC and being provided with a contact number for FESA in Kununurra.

- RacingthePlanet did not contact St John's Ambulance prior to the race despite being advised to do so by the DEC and the KVC.

As a result of those shortcomings in its management and risk assessment, RtP deprived itself of the opportunity to develop relationships with key agencies and individuals that might have been able to provide ongoing assistance and to identify and manage risks that RtP may not have fully understood.[23]

The committee also examined the standards of practice adopted by other adventure racing events organisers operating in remote parts of Australia and found that with respect to RtP's communications and medical and evacuation planning, it did not meet these standards.[24] This finding was based on four key factors:

- RacingthePlanet did not test its communications equipment on the course prior to the race and therefore could not have known if the location of its checkpoints were optimal for communications.
- RacingthePlanet placed its checkpoints too far apart given the limited number of RtP vehicles roving the long course and the inherent difficulties associated with a communication plan based on satellite phones and short-wave radio systems; the committee made particular mention of the inability for sweepers to communicate with checkpoints once out on the course.
- RacingthePlanet did not engage the input and services of St John's Ambulance in Kununurra.

- RacingthePlanet did not make arrangements for the use of a helicopter in an emergency until the day before the event, despite knowing that this would be the only means of evacuation from Tier Gorge. RacingthePlanet designated the helicopter hired by Beyond Action as first responder in the event of an emergency; however it appeared not to have been aware whether this helicopter was appropriately equipped for an emergency evacuation. It did not engage a back-up helicopter.[25]

The committee found that RtP did not take all reasonable steps to maintain the safety of competitors.[26] They based that finding on the following facts:

- Despite RtP being aware of fires in the vicinity of the course in the days leading up to the event, the committee did not receive evidence that RtP had a plan to monitor those fires or detect new fires – other than what could be seen by RtP staff while driving the course – after the race began.
- Before 11 am, RtP's event manager, course director and medical director had all received the message at checkpoint two that a fire was approaching. All failed to hold competitors at the checkpoint while they determined the exact location, direction and severity of the fire referred to in this message.
- RacingthePlanet's event manager and course director met each other on the course approaching checkpoint two shortly after 1 pm. The course director had just sent a volunteer into a potentially dangerous situation in the Tier Gorge – to re-mark the course and assist competitors after seeing smoke in the vicinity of the gorge – without ensuring that the volunteer was carrying communications equipment. Further, this left RtP's operations manager to

continue sweeping the course alone, in contravention of RtP's own risk management plan.

- The event manager was returning from The Barrels where, somewhere between 12.20 pm and 12.40 pm, she had received reports from competitors coming out of the Tier Range of smoke and flames encroaching on the course. Despite this, neither she nor the course director held competitors at checkpoint two while they determined the exact location, direction and severity of the fire.

- With the information available at 1 pm, if not earlier, RtP should have engaged the media helicopter to determine the exact location, direction and severity of the fire and, if required, warn competitors to return to checkpoint two.

- RacingthePlanet's plan to use the Beyond Action helicopter in the case of an emergency (and that it be designated first responder) was neither enacted correctly nor well understood, due in part to the plan having been determined only the day before.[27]

The committee found that had reasonable steps been taken, it was possible that Turia Pitt, Kate Sanderson, Michael Hull, Martin Van der Merwe and Mary Gadams would not have been injured.[28]

The report did not make findings of any legal liability, noting that was the role of an appropriate court.

The committee was asked to examine the roles and actions of various government departments before and during the event. The department which had the greatest responsibility for helping to ensure the event ran smoothly and safely was Tourism WA in its capacity as the sponsor.

Tourism WA told the committee that it considered it particularly important to adopt a standard of 'responsible sponsorship'[29] in the emerging category of adventure sports. The committee examined key tenets of the responsible sponsorship concept as applied to the 2011 Kimberley Ultramarathon and found that Tourism WA and its events agency, Eventscorp, failed to meet their own standards.[30]

The first tenet required the event organiser to demonstrate that it had a competent risk management plan. Tourism WA was found to have signed off on the sponsorship agreement with RtP the day before the event without first viewing its risk management plan. When the plan was shown to Eventscorp's director of events on the same day, according to his submission to the committee, he only 'had a few minutes to mull it over'.[31] A copy of part of the risk management plan was emailed to Eventscorp four days after the event.

Yet Tourism WA had no protocols in place to ensure the plan could have been properly assessed had it been provided in full any earlier – even though a risk management plan that both parties agreed on was one precondition of the milestone payment sponsorship agreement – $20,000 was to be paid on provision of marketing, operations, communications and risk managements plans. In a series of emails between RtP and Eventscorp from 9 to 31 August, neither party made mention of risk management planning.[32]

The committee found serious flaws in Tourism WA's approach to making sure risk management plans for events it sponsored were properly assessed; it appeared all Tourism WA required was that a plan be produced. With RtP a relatively new entrant in the Western Australia market and operating in a remote region, Tourism WA should have been making some effort to have the company prove the adequacy of its risk management plan, the committee said.

'It's not unreasonable to assume that it could have used its event facilitation processes to introduce RtP to the relevant government agencies who could have provided comment and assistance in relation to the company's risk management planning,' the committee reported.[33]

The committee also found that Tourism WA had signed a sponsorship contract without knowing if RtP had the appropriate insurances; Tourism WA confirmed it had not received, assessed or requested the required insurance documents. Tourism WA subsequently requested the insurance certificates for its files from RtP on 9 December 2011, more than three months after the race; it received them on 15 February 2012, more than five months after the race. The insurance certificates were not accompanied by their policies and schedules. Without that documentation the committee had difficulty in determining whether appropriate insurance cover was in place for the injured competitors.[34]

Importantly, clause 15 of the sponsorship agreement stated:

> The Event Holder must provide Tourism WA with information relating to any matter relating to the Agreement within five days of receiving a written request . . . all such information must be full, true and accurate in all aspects to the best of the Event Holder's knowledge at that time.[35]

The committee was not supplied with any documentary evidence that RtP complied with any of the obligations imposed by the sponsorship agreement. However, the committee received advice that the documents presented relating to public liability insurance were '. . . of no apparent value to Tourism WA or to an injured participant'.[36]

In respect of the other documents the committee was advised:

> The worker's compensation 'Notice of Insurance' document appears to be valueless. It is not an insurance contract. The nature of cover is unknown. The Hong Kong insurer presumably is not an Australian Prudential Regulation Authority (APRA) approved insurer and not an approved insurer for the purposes of Workers' Compensation and Injury management Act 1981 (WA). Whether employees of RacingthePlanet are covered for workers' compensation under Hong Kong law if injured in Western Australia is unknown.[37]

Among RtP's documents was a flyer for a medical emergency insurance company – this was of little use to Tourism WA or an injured participant. The committee did not receive any evidence that there was any personal accident insurance cover for volunteers.[38]

Criticisms of other government agencies largely concerned the lines of communication between various parties. While the committee found the onus was on RtP to make contact with relevant agencies (e.g. FESA, DOH, Shire of Wyndham East Kimberley, DEC), after initial direct contact by RtP or when a relevant agency had heard about the event from a third party, not enough effort was put into follow-up investigation of the event and the progress of its organisation.[39]

If FESA, in particular, had been brought into the planning process, the emergency response on the day may have been markedly different; in fact, in the committee's view it may not have been needed as FESA asserted it would have advised RtP to re-route or cancel the race.[40]

The KVC advised FESA's district fire manager about the event three days prior and was told that RtP would be calling for advice on fire. RacingthePlanet was advised by both the KVC and the DEC to contact FESA in Kununurra, and given contact details. The district fire manager was waiting for RtP to make contact but no contact was made. The committee found that when RtP did not make contact, it would have been 'reasonable and prudent' for FESA to contact RtP.[41]

The committee expressed surprise at the way the FESA call centre, Comcen, handled Dr Brandee Waite's initial call from checkpoint two. Dr Waite advised there were people with burns and they needed help with evacuation; at the end of the call she was asked to hang up and call 000 again and request an ambulance service. The committee was of the view that Dr Waite should have been kept on the line while FESA/Comcen organised contact with other relevant emergency services.[42]

The committee found serious failures in sat-phone communications on 2 September;[43] sixty-three emergency phone calls were logged between RtP officials on their satellite phones and various agencies (e.g. FESA, St John's Ambulance, 000) between 2 pm and 8 pm; many of them were recorded as failed calls when the line dropped out before an operator could be reached or during the initial seconds of the call.[44]

The committee made fifteen recommendations.[45] Most were ways various authorities could improve handling of future events, e.g. determining minimum safety standards and improving communications.

Among its recommendations were:

- That Tourism WA revises its sponsorship agreements to ensure that risk management plans are submitted for approval with all relevant agencies and local and State authorities no later than two months prior to a sponsored event, and that milestone payments are linked strictly to this deadline;
- In regard to its due diligence processes for sponsorship agreements, Tourism WA requires event organisers to complete disclosure questionnaires; if an organiser is found at any time not to have complied, or to have withheld material information, penalties should extend to nullifying the contract;
- That Eventscorp ensures that organisers of events it sponsors are directed to all the appropriate authorities and stakeholders;
- All relevant insurance policies and schedules are lodged with Tourism WA by the time a sponsorship agreement is signed and organisers adhere to a clause allowing any claims against them be enforceable in Western Australia or the sponsorship will be withdrawn;
- FESA, WA Police and St John's Ambulance establish a uniform system for handling multiple agency emergency responses that do not involve callers having to make multiple calls to 000;
- That the Western Australian Attorney General gives urgent consideration to an ex-gratia payment to Turia Pitt and Kate Sanderson.

While denying responsibility, the Western Australian Government did make an Act of Grace payment of $450,000 each to Turia and Kate in November 2012. The payment was in recognition of the financial stress of their surgical procedures and medical needs. Deputy Premier, Dr Kim Hames, also mentioned the 'unlikelihood of justice through the court system'.[46] The figure settled on was similar to an amount awarded to a woman recently injured in a helicopter crash.

But by the time of the inquiry's outcome, Turia's medical and associated outgoings had already moved into the millions of dollars; and how can you compensate for a young life tragically altered forever? Greg Walsh continued to pursue justice for Turia from RtP. Finally, in February 2013, Greg received a letter from RtP's lawyers. While RtP remained 'deeply concerned at the serious injuries' Turia sustained, that concern did not lead in any way to legal responsibility for those injuries and it denied liability. Subsequent mediation failed.

On 21 February 2013, Greg filed Turia's statement of claim in the New South Wales Supreme Court. The claim lists a catalogue of omissions by RtP which led to her catastrophic injuries; this included its failure to get advice from the emergency fire authority.

EPILOGUE

FUNDRAISING

Australians nationwide have taken Turia's story to their hearts since it hit the headlines in September 2011. In particular, the close-knit community of Milton–Ulladulla, where Turia grew up, rallied quickly to raise funds to defray her family's considerable expenses.

The first fundraiser was held within weeks of the fire: a local surfing identity, Kurt Nyholm, owner of Milton Akwa Surf, organised a surfing competition at Mollymook Beach. This event raised $20,000.

Later, it became apparent that Turia would live and that her ongoing financial needs would be immense. While the majority of her medical expenses would be covered by Medicare and her health fund, there were other huge ongoing medical and associated costs, such as cosmetic procedures, pressure garments, physiotherapy, occupational therapy, occupational aids, counselling support and day-to-day living expenses during her years of recovery. Turia's debilitating injuries also meant she would be unable to work for some years.

Her two best friends, Kristen Briggs and Nicola Tucker, decided to set up a formal way for people donate. When they were casting about for a charity that might issue the authority to fundraise on Turia's behalf, they came across the Fire Foundation, Australia's only national charity organisation dedicated to supporting fire and burns victims. The foundation was happy to help and, with Turia's consent, set up a trust account in her name to which she had access.

After that, they contacted Go Fundraise, an online fundraising service provider, and asked if it could liaise directly with the Fire Foundation to set up an online donation page for Turia. They agreed and waived their service fee for two years. The online donation page went live in early March 2012 with a target of $100,000. Hundreds of people donated amounts from $25 to more than $3000 and the target was almost reached within a year. Most donors were individuals who wrote moving and encouraging messages with their donations but social clubs, organisations and small businesses also made donations. Many of her former colleagues at the Argyle Mine raised money individually with the Argyle Shave, which required them to shave their heads for money.

The Kununurra community also got into fundraising. Two hundred and twenty locals in this small town turned up for a trivia night which raised $18,000. Included in this amount was the money raised by auctioning naming rights for a crocodile at the Wyndham Crocodile Park. Turia's two friends and former flatmates, Mary Kavanagh and Elle McNamara, were part of a group that chipped in for the winning bid to name the 3-metre croc 'Turia'.

They said they made the purchase in honour of their friend's good sense of humour and to ensure a bit of it remained in the Kimberley. And indeed, when Mary told

Turia about her namesake during her visit to Turia in hospital, Turia loved the idea and had a good laugh. Because crocodiles can live for decades, Turia thought it hilarious that tourists would be asking for many years to come why the croc was called Turia.

Six volunteers from the St John's Ambulance in Kununurra participated in an annual mountain-bike event called the Gibb River Challenge. Seventy teams entered the event, which is held over five days and covers 740 kilometres of the Gibb River Road, an old stock route. Teams use the event to raise funds for their nominated charity; the St John's team raised $33,000, which was divided between Turia and Kate. Another event which raised funds for both Turia and Kate was a fun run in Melbourne in September 2012 organised by one of the competitors in the Kimberley Ultramarathon, Samantha Gash. This event raised $30,000 and brought in another $20,000 in online donations.

But the biggest fundraiser of all was one the whole community of Ulladulla got behind – the masquerade ball in the local civic centre hall on 5 May 2012. It was a sell-out, with more than 500 people paying $60 a ticket to attend; many others who couldn't attend bought 'virtual tickets' online for $40 each. The total raised on the night was more than $60,000. The Macquarie Foundation matched one-third of the night's proceeds, kicking in an additional $20,000.

The ball was the brainchild of Kristen and Nicola and they chose a masked event in deference to Turia having to wear a compression mask; they wanted her to feel comfortable, even though they knew she would only be able to attend for a short time. It was a major event for the two young women to organise but they were fortunate to win the support of everyone they approached. Once they worked out what needed to be supplied, such as catering, alcohol, decorations, lighting, sound, entertainment, raffle prizes and auction items, they contacted everyone they knew who could help or point them in the direction of someone who could.

A friend who was a chef organised the catering; another friend's father owned a bottle shop and he organised the alcohol; decorations were done by local girlfriends; businesses in the surrounding district donated items to raffle or for the live auctions. The highlight of the auctions was a diamond donated by Rio Tinto, owners of the Argyle Diamond Mine, where Turia had been working.

A photo booth was set up where people could pay $5 to have their photos taken – one to keep and one to go into a memory book for Turia. People who bought virtual tickets were asked to send a photo of themselves; these were printed and pasted on balloons which became part of the decorations; the balloons were photographed and sent to each virtual guest so they could see what a great night their virtual self had enjoyed.

Turia used this money to fund her trip to the specialist burns clinic, the Ster Centre in France, in March 2013.

In the weeks following the fire, Turia's family was overwhelmed by the generosity of so many people. Michael Pitt was moved to write a letter to the *Milton Ulladulla Times*:

Thank you from the Pitt Family of Ulladulla. Thank you to the wonderful people of this great town. The well wishes, kind thoughts, offers of help as well as donations from so many of you have touched our hearts as a family. You all need to know that this has been an inspiration to Turia as she faces the greatest challenge of her life. She is conscious, aware, positive, and progressing well with her recovery.

Fundraising

To all those who have been involved in saving Turia's life, we can never thank you enough.

The fellow runners who found, and attended to Turia and Kate at the scene of the accident, and who ran for help; the courageous and skilled helicopter pilot who airlifted the girls out; the paramedic and St John's Ambulance volunteers who attended the girls; the Royal Flying Doctor Service who flew the girls to Darwin General Hospital, and Careflight, who flew them on to Sydney and Melbourne. The staff of both Darwin General Hospital and the skilled surgeons, nurses and staff of Concord General Repatriation Hospital.

And thank you to those who helped, but are not on this list. Thank you to everyone for your continued fundraising activities and support for this special lady.

Great people.

Great town . . .

How good is Australia.

www.firefoundation.org.au/
http://supportturiapitt.gofundraise.com.au/page/turia

Michael Pitt

ABOUT SKIN DONATION

Most people are aware that hundreds of lives are saved every year by donated organs. People tick the boxes for organs they know can be transplanted, such as kidneys, heart, lungs, corneas – but few people realise that donated skin can also save lives, so it remains in short supply in Australia. On average, skin from three donors is needed for one recipient, and currently Australia can neither meet the immediate demand for skin nor stockpile it for use in the event of major disasters, such as bush fires and terrorist bombings like the Bali bombings in 2002.

With an average total surface of about 1.8 m^2 and a total weight of about 11 kilograms, skin is our largest organ. Apart from giving us our appearance and shape, it has other important functions, such as regulating our body temperature and protecting us from the environmental impact of chemicals, the sun's UV radiation and bacteria. Skin also provides us with one of our most important senses – that of touch. This is made possible by cells and nerve endings in the skin which send impulses to our central nervous system.

Most recipients of donor skin are burn victims and the skin grafts are used as a sort of temporary bandage. The donated skin helps to decrease pain, acts as a barrier to infection, prevents fluid and protein loss, and helps regulate body temperature. As in Turia's case, donated skin can be used as a temporary treatment to cover severe burns and infected areas while the patient's own skin heals. It promotes healing of underlying tissue and provides excellent wound cover till the patient's own donor skin sites become ready for re-harvesting. The skin eventually sloughs off or is removed after a few weeks.

While skin and tissue donation is far less common or well known than organ donation, many more would-be donors meet the criteria to provide skin. Whereas organ donation requires the very specific circumstance of clinical brain death, combined with continued respiratory and circulatory support, there are few medical conditions that rule out tissue donation. Exceptions would be transmissible diseases such as hepatitis and HIV.

Transplanting donated skin also differs from organ transplantation as the skin grafts are used to provide temporary protection and are not expected to survive in the recipient permanently. This means that neither ABO blood group nor HLA matching is required for allograft skin transplantation. So literally anyone can be a donor for anyone else.

The decision to donate skin is made in the same manner as other organ donations and does not affect the medical care given to the donor before death. Donating skin does not cause body disfigurement; the skin harvested is a very thin layer, a bit like the skin that peels off after sunburn and is taken from the abdomen, back and legs; it can be donated up to twenty-four hours after death.

Skin is not the only tissue that can be donated after death and anyone can be considered for suitability as a tissue donor. Other tissues that can be donated include:

- *Eyes* can help restore sight to people with cornea problems, which may result from eye disease or injury or birth defects; the white part of the eye (the sclera) can be used in operations to rebuild the eye.

- *Heart valves* can be transplanted to help save the lives of children born with heart defects and adults with damaged heart valves.
- *Bone* has an important use in artificial joint replacements or replacing bone that has been removed due to illness or injury. It helps reduce pain and improves mobility.
- *Tendons*, the elastic-like cords that attach bones and muscles to each other, can help rebuild damaged joints.

The concept of skin donation after death is not new and there have been enormous developments in the field of tissue transplants over the last fifty years. The discovery of the protective properties of glycerol and its ability to maintain the cell structure unaltered led to the establishment of tissue banks throughout the world. Their aim was to collect, treat and distribute tissues. Skin can also be preserved by freezing, which, unlike storage in glycerol, maintains cell viability.

The first proper skin bank was established by the United States Navy in 1949. Subsequently many others, mostly multi-tissue banks, were established across the country. Today the American Association of Transplant Banks has around fifty accredited skin-tissue banks. The first tissue bank in the UK was established in Yorkshire in 1960. The Netherlands established a skin bank in 1976 and further evolution of techniques to preserve skin led to the opening of the Euro Skin Bank in 1992. This bank distributes homologous skin to more than thirty burns centres throughout Europe. The Euro Skin Bank is regulated by European directives, national legislation and internal protocols; it collects, qualifies, processes, cryo-preserves and distributes bone and skin taken from brain-dead donors. The tissue bank is also involved in education, scientific research, training and the development of a donation culture in the community.

Italy currently has five tissue banks that store skin and Canada has four. With improvements of the health sector in many developing countries in the last thirty years, more and more patients have been treated using sterilised tissues imported from developed countries; but the cost of this is high, significantly increasing the cost of treatment for burns and other conditions, such as leprosy, intractable skin wounds and pressure-sore ulcers. With the support of many developed countries, skin banks have been gradually set up in developing regions; there are now sixty-six tissue banks in the Asia-Pacific. The first tissue bank in Latin America was set up in Argentina in 1993 and there are currently thirty-seven tissue banks in seven countries of the region. There are seven countries in Africa with tissue banks.

Australia's small population means it is not considered cost efficient to have a separate skin bank in every state. The Donor Tissue Bank of Victoria (DTBV) is the country's main source of donated skin. It is run by the Victorian Institute of Forensic Medicine attached to Monash University and specialises in the collection of human tissues such as heart valves, skin, bone and corneas. Established in 1989, the DTBV was the first, and remains the only, multi-tissue bank in Australasia. It is also Australia's only tissue bank which screens donors, processes, stores, tests and distributes multiple types of tissue from the one facility. It is a public-sector, not-for-profit organisation and its main function is providing Australian surgeons with safe and effective tissue grafts for transplantation in many areas of orthopaedic, cardiothoracic, reconstructive surgery and burn care.

The only other skin bank in Australia is the Queensland Skin Bank, which opened in 2008 and is based at the Royal Brisbane and Women's Hospital Burns Unit. It is divided into two services: the Queensland Skin Culture Centre, which takes small samples of undamaged skin from the patient and grows the top layer (epidermis) from the patient's own skin cells and returns it to the patient to permanently cover their burn wounds; the other service is the skin bank, which stores allograft skin (donor skin) from deceased tissue donors.

In her effort to promote awareness of skin donation, Turia and has become an unofficial ambassador for Donate Life, the Australian Government's Organ and Tissue Authority. The authority, an independent statutory body, was established in 2009 as part of a government reform package to bring world's best practice to *organ and tissue donation for transplantation*. The government believed its reform program would provide an unprecedented opportunity to transform and save more Australian lives.

The authority's aim was to set up a partnership with States, Territories, clinicians, consumers and the community to bring a nationally coordinated approach to organ and tissue donation. It is also responsible for administering funds to non-government organisations for essential associated services.

To register to be considered for donation and to be included on an Australia-wide computer database or for more information, visit the DonateLife website www. donatelife.gov.au/.

Facts about organ and tissue donation in Australia[1]
- One organ and tissue donor can transform the lives of 10 or more people.

- Australia is a world leader for successful transplant outcomes.
- Around 1600 people are on Australian organ transplant waiting lists.
- To lift donation rates the Australian Government, with State and Territory governments, has implemented a national reform package, 'A World's Best Practice Approach to Organ and Tissue Donation for Transplantation'.
- In 2012, 354 organ donors gave 1052 Australians a new chance in life.
- The number of organ donors and transplant recipients in 2012 was the highest since national records began.
- 80 per cent of Australians are generally willing to become organ donors and 78 per cent are willing to become tissue donors.
- Only around 1 per cent of people actually die in hospital in the specific circumstances where organ donation is possible. The circumstances in which someone can become a tissue donor are less limited.
- In Australia the family will always be asked to confirm the donation wishes of the deceased before donation can proceed.
- Less than 60 per cent of families in Australia give consent for organ and tissue donation to proceed.
- 44 per cent of Australians do not know or are not sure of the donation wishes of their loved ones.
- 92 per cent of Australians who are aware of their family members' wishes indicate that they would uphold those wishes.
- 81 per cent of Australians recognise it is important to discuss their donation wishes with the people close to them.
- 77 per cent of Australians have now discussed their donation wishes with their family.

While Australia is recognised as a world leader in transplantation medicine, the number of organ and tissue donations in Australia is low by global standards. Skin donation wasn't something Turia Pitt had ever given any thought to before the donated skin flown from California saved her life. Turia is now on a mission to raise public awareness and encourage more people to consider putting skin on their list of donated organs.

NOTES

On 1 March 2012 the Legislative Assembly of Western Australia directed The Economics and Industry Standing Committee to investigate and report on the 2011 Kimberley Ultramarathon event. This included investigating whether RacingthePlanet had taken all reasonable steps to identify and reduce risks and maintain the safety of competitors, employees, contractors, spectators and volunteers in the preparation for and the running of the event and in responding to the fire and the injuries, including access to medical support and evacuations. It also included investigating the role of various WA Government departments and agencies in connection with the event and the protection and rescue of the individuals concerned.

On 16 August 2012, the chair of the committee tabled with the Legislative Assembly the 294-page report: *Report Number 13 – Inquiry into the 2011 Kimberly Ultramarathon* (hereafter referred to as Inquiry Report). In September 2012, the committee resolved that all evidence, submissions in communications should be tabled unless it consisted of evidence taken in camera or where contributors requested that material not be tabled or where it was information relating to a personal nature. The Inquiry Report is available at: www.parliament.wa.gov.au/parliament/commit.nsf/all/ F75A6BCD99B1746848257A5C000A0160?opendocument

Transcripts of evidence are available at:

www.parliament.wa.gov.au/parliament/commit.nsf/
CommitSearchView?SearchView&Query=kimberley%20
ultramarathon

Chapter Two: Michael

1 Sponsorship Agreement, Western Australian Tourism Commission and Racing the Planet Events Limited 30 August 2011, tabled at Inquiry 26 March 2012.

Chapter Three: The Run-up

1 Andrew Baker, volunteer, Police Statement, 17 September, 2011, p. 2; Hal Benson, competitor, Police Statement, 7 September, 2011, p. 2; Bradley Bull, competitor, Police Statement, 12 September, 2011, p. 2; Lon Croot, volunteer, Police Statement, 5 September, 2011, p. 2; Ellis Gaffin, competitor, Police Statement, 7 September, 2011, p. 2; Michael Hull, competitor, Police Statement, 8 September 2011, p. 3; Turia Pitt, competitor, transcript of evidence, 30 April, 2012, p. 15, Kate Sanderson, competitor, transcript of evidence, 30 April, 2012, p. 14; Heather Scott, competitor, Police Statement, 6 September, 2011, p. 1; Shaun Van der Merwe, competitor, transcript of evidence, 30 April, 2012, p. 14; Inquiry Report pp. 14, 15, 64, 65.

Chapter Six: Delay

1 Inquiry Report pp. 14, 15.
2 Ibid.
3 Inquiry Report p. 15.
4 Mr John Storey – Supplementary Item A – Response to Questions on Notice.

5 Inquiry Report, p. 68.

6 Appendix 2 (Statement to Police, paras 32, 33) of Written Submission of Mr John Storey on 19 Mar 2012.

7 Inquiry Report, p. 69; Written Submission of Mr Nathan Summers on 15 May 2012.

8 Inquiry Report, p. 80.

9 Ibid.

10 Ibid.

11 Ibid.

12 Inquiry Report, pp. 80–81, 86.

13 Inquiry Report, pp. 86, 87.

14 Ibid.

15 Inquiry Report, pp. 86, 87.

16 Andrew Baker, volunteer, Police Statement, 17 September, 2011, p. 2; Hal Benson, competitor, Police Statement, 7 September, 2011, p. 2; Bradley Bull, competitor, Police Statement, 12 September, 2011, p. 2; Lon Croot, volunteer, Police Statement, 5 September, 2011, p. 2; Ellis Caffin, competitor, Police Statement, 7 September, 2011, p. 2; Michael Hull, competitor, Police Statement, 8 September 2011, p. 3; Turia Pitt, competitor, transcript of evidence, 30 April, 2012, p. 15, Kate Sanderson, competitor, transcript of evidence, 30 April, 2012, p. 14; Heather Scott, competitor, Police Statement, 6 September, 2011, p. 1; Shaun Van der Merwe, competitor, transcript of evidence, 30 April, 2012, p. 14; Inquiry Report pp. 14, 15, 64, 65.

Chapter Seven: Miscommunications

1 Inquiry Report, pp. 219–21.

2 Inquiry Report, pp. viii, xxi, 222.

3 Inquiry Report, pp. 94–95.

4 Inquiry Report, p. 95.

5 Ibid.

6 Inquiry Report, pp. ii–iii, 56–57, 63.

7 Inquiry Report, p. 93.

8 Inquiry Report, p. 97.

Chapter Eight: Rescue

1 Paul Cripps Police Statement, 5 September 2011.

2 Inquiry Report pp. 100–101.

3 Transcript courtesy Heliworks WA.

Chapter Seventeen: The Ripple Effect

1 Transcript of Evidence, 24/2/2012.

2 Heather Scott, Statement to Police, 6/9/11.

Chapter Eighteen: Holding Responsibility

1 Inquiry report, p. 4.

2 Ibid.

3 See Inquiry Report, pp. 47–49.

4 *Hansard 21 February 2011.*

5 Ibid.

6 Ibid.

7 Ibid.

8 Inquiry Report, p. i.

9 Inquiry Report, p, 156.

10 Ibid.

11 Transcript of evidence, 02/05/2012, pp. 3, 5.

12 Transcript of evidence, 02/05/2012, p. 11.

13 Transcript of evidence, 02/05/2012, p. 17.

14 Ibid.

15 Ibid.

16 'Kimberley race founder Mary Gadams denies liability for burned competitors', Lisa MacNamara, *The Australian*, 16 August 2012.

17 Ibid.

18 Ibid.

19 Inquiry Report pages 14, 15.

20 Transcript of Evidence, 24/2/2012.

21 Inquiry Report, pp. xiii–iv.

22 Inquiry Report, p. xiii.

23 Ibid.

24 Inquiry Report, p. xiv.

25 Ibid.

26 Ibid.

27 Inquiry Report, p. xv.

28 Ibid.

29 Inquiry Report, p. 155.

30 Ibid.

31 Inquiry Report, p. 159.

32 Inquiry Report, pp. 159–60.

33 Inquiry Report, p. 160.

34 Report Inquiry p. 167.

35 Report Inquiry p. 166.

36 Report Inquiry p. 165.

37 Report Inquiry pp. 166–66.

38 Report Inquiry p. 166.

39 Inquiry Report, pp vii–x, xxii.

40 Inquiry Report, p. 217.

41 Report Inquiry, pp. vii–viii.

42 Inquiry Report, p. viii.

43 Inquiry Report, p. xiv.

44 Inquiry, Index to Evidence.

45 Inquiry Report, pp xviii–xxiv.

46 'Kimberley fire victims to get $450,000 each', Courtney Trenwith, *The Sydney Morning Herald*, 14/11/12.

About Skin Donation

1   Statistics from DonateLife.

PICTURE CREDITS

The authors and publisher are grateful to the following individuals for permission to use their photographs:

Kristen Briggs: friends in Queenstown, New Zealand.
Karisa McCauley: masquerade ball.
Natalie Osmetti/St John's Ambulance: Tier Gorge.

All other photographs courtesy Pitt family.

ACKNOWLEDGEMENTS

TURIA PITT

There are so many people to thank, so I'll start with everyone who was involved in my initial survival. The boys from Newcrest – Trent Breen, Brad Bull and Wade Dixon. Sarel de Koker and Bonny Rugendyke for treating me as best they could on the scene. Paul Cripps, the extraordinary helicopter pilot. The entire team at the Darwin Hospital. My fellow runners who were caught in the fire: Hal Benson, Michael Hull, Kate Sanderson and Shaun and Martin Van de Merwe. We are all survivors.

I'd also like to thank everyone at the Concord Repatriation General Hospital: my incredibly skilled surgeons, Professor Peter Haertsch and Professor Peter Maitz. Superlatives are not enough to describe you. Despite the pain they inflicted, my physiotherapists Frank Li, Lexie Barwick and Orla McDonnell. My innovative occupational therapists, Cheree Walker and Jessica Allchin. My favourite anaesthetist, Kar-Soon Lim. The two handsome burns registrars – Dr James and Dr Sam. The three empathetic clinical nurses – Rae Johnson, Tom Leuong and Sue Taggart. The entire nursing staff, including Penny Gutierrez, Naresh Kar, Jiggy Kiriya, Susan Lian, Melissa Meadows, Tama Miller, Chris Parker and James Scott.

There are so many positive things that happened after the fire. I'd like to thank Michael Usher, for telling my story the way I wanted it to be told. The delightful Ali Smith, a wonderful producer who has also become a close mate. Slabber van Deventer, Giles Lenz, Mischa Mann and Glenn Roberts – my understanding bosses at Rio Tinto. Greg Walsh, a bulldog of a lawyer who thankfully is in my corner. Ian Sanderson, for his dogged determination for justice. Sophie Ambrose, for initiating this book. And finally, my ghostwriter, Libby Harkness: you have done such a brilliant job. Thank you, thank you, thank you.

I would like to thank everyone who has been involved in my rehabilitation in Ulladulla: My physiotherapist, Janine Austen, for being there since the beginning. My personal trainer, Emily Bingham, for pushing me when I need it. My general practitioner, Herbert Chee, for filling out endless certificates, forms and scripts. My psychologist, Jennifer Clarke, for teaching me how to think rationally. Gym owner Lloyd Egan, for showing me my inner strength. My exercise physiologist ,Gregg Orphin, for helping me to get back into the water. My masseuse, Nicola Parnell, for imparting to me the power of relaxation. Finally my yoga instructor, Himani Smeaton – I have come so far under your tutelage.

Thank you to all my fantastic friends: Mary Kavanagh, for always making the effort to see me. Kristen Briggs, for your wicked sense of humour. Nicola Tucker, for helping me stay on top of things and always encouraging me. Shae Clayton, for understanding me despite being ridiculously random. Thanks also to Melanie Basile, Nina Best, Julia Hasche, Kate McKutcheon, Sarah Montefiore and Tess Wilson.

I'd also like to thank my entire extended family: Uncle Insect (Ian Pitt) and Maria Pitt, for letting us use their beach house for extended periods of time. Uncle Westie (Andrew

Pitt) and Terri Janke, for their ongoing legal advice and support. Megsie (Margaret Pitt), for her weekly letters and chocolates. Genji and Angela Pitt, for their hospitality. Thanks also to Shay Bogg, Aaron and Rachel Hoskin, Patricia Hooke and Monsieur (Alan Pitt) and Mamie (Viola Vaite).

I'd like to thank Dad (Michael Pitt) for taking charge of all things fitness as well as being so tech-savvy. My younger brothers, Heimanu and Toriki Pitt, for always making me laugh and giving me brotherly cuddles. Shae Hoskin, for being such a beautiful sister-in-law – thank you for the walks, laughs and educated discussions. Julie and Gary Hoskin, for treating me like their own daughter. Words cannot express how grateful I am. Thank you John Maguire, for being Mum's rock. And finally, to the two people to whom this book is dedicated: Michael Hoskin and Mum (Celestine Vaite). You both have made this journey so much easier. I am blessed to have both of you.

ACKNOWLEDGEMENTS

LIBBY HARKNESS

I would like to thank the many people who contributed in some way to the writing of Turia's story. Involving as it did the input from many different people, it was a difficult story to pull together; everyone had a version of events and while I tried my best to accurately mesh them all together, some things were just unknowable.

First, thanks to Michael Hoskin, Turia's loving and supportive partner, for putting his pain second in every telling of her journey; Célestine, the third amigo, who wept and laughed in equal measures during our interviews; Heimanu and Toriki for the letters; Genji for his forthrightness; Michael Pitt, who spoke of justice for his golden girl; and Gary and Julie Hoskin for their quiet dignity.

Writing about what happened that day would not have been possible without the input and generous help of the other five who survived with Turia on the ridge: Kate Sanderson, Michael Hull, Hal Benson and Shaun and Martin Van der Merwe, each of whom related their own moving recollections – Shaun above the din at Perth International Airport and Martin via email from Ghana. The Newcrest miners: Bradley Bull, for breaking the silence 'for Turia', Wade Dixon and Trent Breen for photos.

The other Kununurra heroes: helicopter pilot Paul Cripps from Heliwork WA, who flew me over the Kimberley region so I could see for myself where it happened; his co-pilot, Bryn Watson, for his 'patter'; St John's paramedic Sarel De Koker, who gave me a vivid description of the rescue; and helicopter pilot Nathan Summers, who gave me details by phone from a remote region in Western Australia.

Race event volunteers Lon Croot and Scott Connell, and competitors Ellis Caffin, Heather Scott and Rod Rutherford, each of whom relived their nightmares of that day for me. *The Kimberley Echo* in Kununurra, which allowed me to rummage around their back issues. The Kimberleyland Holiday Park, which gave me a cute cabin overlooking the lake to stay in while I was in Kununurra. Natalie Osmetti for photos of the helicopter rescue.

Michelle Foster at the National Critical Care and Trauma Response Centre at Royal Darwin Hospital, who put me in touch with those who treated Turia and Kate in Darwin – Mr Shiby Ninan, Dr Gabrielle Weidmann, critical care nurse Belinda Nolan, and Dr Steven Hudson, who spoke to me from New Zealand – all of whom remembered clearly the events of the day Turia and the others were admitted.

Turia's surgeons at Sydney's Concord Hospital, Professor Peter Maitz and Professor Peter Haertsch, who gave me hours of their valuable time; Janine Austen for the physiotherapy (mine and Turia's); Kristen Briggs for the insights into Turia's life before the fire; Ali Smith from *60 Minutes*, who shared her material, and Michael Usher for his foreword; Greg Walsh, who cast his legal eye over the manuscript.

Thanks to Sophie Ambrose (at Random House) for introducing me to Turia, who although still fragile, was enthusiastic to tell her story. I also want to thank my marathon-runner friend Michael Brosnan, who, when I said I was worried about finding time to write this book replied: 'You have to find time; you must write Turia's story.' And my editor, Anne Reilly, who asked the right questions. A special thanks to Ian Sanderson, without whose dogged efforts the Western Australian Government Inquiry into the 2011 Ultramarathon would not have happened and who shared with me information I could not have got elsewhere. I am also grateful to Ian and Maria Pitt, who let me live in their peaceful Ulladulla beach house while I wrote.

And last and by no means least, I want to thank Turia for allowing me to write her story and putting me straight about the sort of book she wanted at our first meeting when she said, 'I don't want a boring book.'

ABOUT THE AUTHORS

Turia Pitt has a double degree in Mining Engineering and Science. She worked as a model before landing her dream job with Rio Tinto at their prestigious Argyle Diamond Mine and moving to Kununurra with her partner, Michael. Their lives were turned upside down when she was trapped by a grassfire in a 100-kilometre ultramarathon in September 2011, and suffered burns to sixty-five per cent of her body.

For now, she is living in her hometown of Ulladulla, surrounded by friends and family. She spends her time at physiotherapy, the gym, and is studying for her Masters.

www.turiapitt.com
www.twitter.com/PittTuria

Libby Harkness is a non-fiction writer and published author of many books. Her published works include a number of 'firsts'. The acclaimed *Looking for Lisa* (Random House 1991) was the first book internationally on adoption reunions between biological mothers and their relinquished children; her book *Skin Deep* (Random House 1994) was the first in-depth look at the plastic/cosmetic surgery industry to be published in Australia and Canada.

Today, Libby is a specialist life-story writer and one of Australia's leading ghostwriters. Among her most recent work is *The Widow* with Nola Duncan (Random House 2013). New Zealand-born Libby lives in Sydney and has four adult children.

www.writerforhire.com.au